Principles of
Home Decoration

DINING-ROOM IN "PENNYROYAL" (IN MRS. BOUDINOT KEITH'S COTTAGE, ONTEORA)

Principles of Home Decoration

With Practical Examples

By

Candace Wheeler

Applewood Books
Bedford, Massachusetts

Principles of Home Decoration was first published in 1903 by Doubleday, Page & Company of New York.

Thank you for purchasing an Applewood Book. Applewood reprints America's lively classics—books from the past that are still of interest to modern readers. For a free copy of our current catalog, please write to Applewood Books, P.O. Box 365, Bedford, MA 01730.

ISBN 1-55709-497-7

Library of Congress Catalog Card Number: 00-105703

2 4 6 8 10 9 7 5 3 1

CONTENTS

CONTENTS *(Continued)*

LIST OF ILLUSTRATIONS

LIST OF ILLUSTRATIONS (*Continued*)

INTRODUCTION

MEN designed America's high-style interiors, until 1879 when Louis Comfort Tiffany asked Candace Thurber Wheeler (1827–1923) to join him, Samuel Colman, and Lockwood de Forest at Associated Artists. The firm treated decoration as a fine art and decorated important buildings, such as New York City's Seventh Regiment Armory, and elegant residences, including Mark Twain's home and the White House. By 1883, when the firm disbanded, Wheeler had a national reputation for innovative embroidery, textile, and color design. While her former partners pursued their arts, Mrs. Wheeler, as clients and the press called her, had a very different agenda. She continued Associated Artists, but set out to improve the only sphere then controlled by women, the ordinary American home. In 1903, Wheeler published a popular how-to book, *Principles of Home Decoration*, devoted entirely to modest houses.

Principles of Home Decoration would become a standard text recommended for use in schools. It owed its existence to the English-born Aesthetic

Movement, which transformed American homes in the last third of the nineteenth century. Aesthetes such as Oscar Wilde and James McNeill Whistler believed that beauty improves the beholder by stimulating the creative imagination and feelings. A well-designed "artistic home" full of tasteful wallpapers, fabrics, furniture, and collections of natural and art objects shaped inhabitants by surrounding them with beauty. In the parlor of Wheeler's summer cottage, a hand-painted frieze proclaims: "Who Creates a Home Creates a Potent Spirit Which in Turn Doth Fashion Him That Fashioned." Decorating was both an art and a means to self-improvement.

For Wheeler, Aesthetic ideas resonated deeply. She spent 32 years as a homemaker and mother of four children before taking up design. Candace Thurber grew up in Delhi, in rural New York State. She moved to New York City when she married Thomas Wheeler, who became a successful wharf broker. The Wheeler's home was truly artistic. Their friends included the painters Frederic E. Church, Samuel F. B. Morse, Eastman Johnson, and Albert Bierstadt. Wheeler herself became known for her paintings of flowers.

While the artistic home strove for elegance, Wheeler saw its democratic implications. "It is by no means an unimportant thing to create a beautiful and picturesque interior," she observed in *Principles of Home Decoration*. "There is no influence so potent upon life as harmonious surroundings, and to create and possess a home which is harmonious in a simple and inexpensive way is the privilege of all but the wretchedly poor." Wheeler recognized that most Americans lived in builders' houses and apartments, often renting, not owning, their homes. *Principles of Home Decoration* proposed to reform society, one family at a time, by improving these humble surroundings.

Wheeler's interest in reform began in 1876, when her older daughter died unexpectedly. In crisis, she vowed to use her talents and social position to improve the lot of women. Wheeler founded the Society of Decorative Arts to teach women design and then the Women's Exchange, to market their products. Thanks to the Society, she tried her hand at design and met Tiffany. At age 52, she joined Associated Artists.

As the firm's textile specialist, Wheeler experimented with inexpensive fabrics. Once she headed Associated Artists, she focused its energies on designing prize-winning wallpapers and fabrics for commercial manufacture. Critics praised her for producing the first affordable products with a distinctively American look.

Wheeler also practiced cost-effective decorating. She designed cottages for Onteora, a community she founded in the Catskills. *Principles of Home Decoration* presented principles Wheeler tested in these simple buildings, illustrated by photographs of their interiors. The black-and-white photographs barely suggested her results, which relied heavily on color. Her principles treated color as a room's cheapest and most powerful source of atmosphere.

Colors and all decorative materials must harmonize with their contexts. For Wheeler, all design depended on "the great law of appropriateness." A room's color should suit its natural light and even the colors of the landscape outside it. A beach house's fabrics should feature seashells, not woodland flowers.

Wheeler found universal principles "by tracing back sensation to its source, and finding out why certain things are utterly satisfactory, and certain others a positive source of discomfort." In *Principles of Home Decoration* she argued that the feel of a house arises from pleasing design patterns. Her own design favored cozy inglenooks, low-ceilinged rooms juxtaposed with double-height ones, second-floor galleries, fireplaces, and exquisite color combinations based on ordinary fabrics. All of Wheeler's principles put the inhabitant's experience and satisfaction first. They anticipated by 75 years the person-centered "pattern language" design advanced by theorist Christopher Alexander.

Wheeler believed she had first-hand information about traditional patterns that satisfied. In her 1918 autobiography, *Yesterdays In A Busy Life*, she maintained that her family's home had not changed since the eighteenth century, that she had actually grown up in an early American home. Wheeler helped shape the emerging Colonial Revival, which advocated a new old-fashioned home based on sincerity and simplicity. *Principles of Home Decoration* was a manual for Colonial Revival decoration—but one based on traditional principles, rather than on precious antiques.

In *The Cosmopolitan* magazine, in 1889, Elizabeth Bisland described Wheeler's "large, low living-room": "The walls are covered with coarse palmetto matting from the West Indies . . . . (T)he room is hung and the divans and tables covered with the same blue denim, which, with its reverse sides, dark blue and blue-gray, gives charming results for an almost inappreciable expense. The tall dresser is filled with blue willow-pattern china . . . . In the corner is a big open fireplace, and the furniture is all of the local make, stained brown."

Bisland could be describing the interiors illustrated in today's glossy shelter magazines and home-furnishing catalogues. Wheeler popularized hardwood floors, tone-on-tone rugs with bold borders, light wall colors, subtle wallpapers, furnished kitchens hung with gleaming pots and pans, tall-ceilinged great rooms, stenciled wall-decoration, and washable fabrics.

Fittingly, since *Principles of Home Decoration*'s third (and last) printing, in 1913, her reform style has become comfortable modern style. Whether it be a clapboard Victorian cottage or a vinyl-sided townhouse, Candace Wheeler set out to make the home delightful.

–JEAN DUNBAR, June 27, 2000

Principles of
Home Decoration

Principles of Home Decoration

CHAPTER I

DECORATION AS AN ART

"Who creates a Home, creates a potent spirit which in turn doth fashion him that fashioned."

PROBABLY no art has so few masters as that of decoration. In England, Morris was for many years the great leader, but among his followers in England no one has attained the dignity of unquestioned authority; and in America, in spite of far more general practice of the art, we still are without a leader whose very name establishes law.

It is true we are free to draw inspiration from the same sources which supplied Morris and the men associated with him in his enthusiasms, and in fact we do lean, as they did, upon English eighteenth-century domestic art—and derive from the men who made that period famous many of our articles of faith ; but there are almost no authoritative books upon the subject of appropriate modern decoration.   Our text books are still to be written ; and one must glean knowledge from many sources, shape it into rules, and test the rules, before adopting them as safe guides.

Yet in spite of the absence of authoritative teaching, we have learned that an art dependent upon other arts, as decoration is upon building and architecture, is bound to follow the principles which govern them.   We must base our work upon what has already been done, select our decorative forms from appropriate periods, conform our use of colour to the principles of colour, and be able to choose and apply all manufactures in accordance with the great law of appropriateness.   If we do this, we stand upon something capable of evolution and the creation of a system.

In so far as the principles of decoration are derived from other arts, they can be acquired by every one, but an exquisite feeling in their application is the distinguishing quality of the true decorator.

There is quite a general impression that house-decoration is not an art which requires a long course of study and training, but some kind of natural knack of arrangement — a faculty of making things "look pretty," and that any one who has this faculty is amply qualified for "taking up house-decoration." Indeed, natural facility succeeds in satisfying many personal cravings for beauty, although it is not competent for general practice.

Of course there are people, and many of them, who are gifted with an inherent sense of balance and arrangement, and a true eye for colour, and—given the same materials—such people will make a room pleasant and cozy, where one without these gifts would make it positively ugly. In so far, then, individual gifts are a great advantage, yet one possessing them in even an unusual degree may make great mistakes in decoration. What *not* to do, in this day of almost universal experiment, is perhaps the most valuable lesson to the untrained decorator. Many of the rocks upon which he splits are down in no chart, and lie in the track of what seems to him perfectly plain sailing.

There are houses of fine and noble exterior which are vulgarized by uneducated experiments in colour and ornament, and belittled by being filled with heterogeneous collections of unimportant art. Yet these very instances serve to emphasize the demand for beautiful surroundings, and in spite of mistakes and incongruities, must be reckoned as efforts toward a desirable end.

In spite of a prevalent want of training, it is astonishing how much we have of good interior decoration, not only in houses of great importance, but in those of people of average fortunes—indeed, it is in the latter that we get the general value of the art.

This comparative excellence is to be referred to the very general acquirement of what we call "art cultivation" among American women, and this, in conjunction with a knowledge that her social world will be apt to judge of her capacity by her success or want of success in making her own surroundings beautiful, determines the efforts of the individual woman. She feels that she is expected to prove her superiority by living in a home distinguished for beauty as well as for the usual orderliness and refinement. Of course this sense of obligation is a powerful spur to the exercise of natural gifts, and if in addition to these she has the habit of reasoning upon the principles of things, and is sufficiently cultivated in the literature of art to avoid unwarrantable experiment, there is no reason why she should not be successful in her own surroundings.

The typical American, whether man or woman, has great natural facility, and when the fact is once recognized that beauty—like education—can dignify any circumstances, from the narrowest to the most opulent, it becomes one of the objects of life to secure it. *How* this is done depends upon the talent and cultivation of the family, and this is often adequate for excellent results.

It is quite possible that so much general ability may discourage the study of decoration as a precise form of art, since it encourages the idea that The House Beautiful can be secured by any one who has money to pay for processes, and possesses what is simply designated as " good taste."

We do not find this impulse toward the creation of beautiful interiors as noticeable in other countries as in America. The instinct of self-expression is much stronger in us than in other races, and for that reason we cannot be contented with the utterances of any generation, race or country save our own. We gather to ourselves what we personally enjoy or wish to enjoy, and will not take our domestic environment at second hand. It follows that there is a certain difference and originality in our methods, which bids fair to acquire distinct character, and may in the future distinguish this art-loving period as a maker of style.

A successful foreign painter who has visited this country at intervals during the last ten years said, "There is no such uniformity of beautiful interiors anywhere else in the world. There are palaces in France and Italy, and great country houses in England, to the embellishment of which generations of owners have devoted the best art of their own time; but in America there is something of it everywhere. Many unpretentious houses have drawing-rooms possessing colour-decoration which would distinguish them as examples in England or France."

To Americans this does not seem a remarkable fact. We have come into a period which desires beauty, and each

one secures it as best he can. We are a
teachable and a studious people, with a
faculty of turning " general information "
to account; and general information
upon art matters has had much to do
with our good interiors.

We have, perhaps half unconsciously,
applied fundamental principles to our
decoration, and this may be as much
owing to natural good sense as to cultivation. We have a habit of reasoning
about things, and acting upon our con-
clusions, instead of allowing the rest of
the world to do the reasoning while we
adopt the result. It is owing to this
conjunction of love for and cultivation
of art, and the habit of materializing
what we wish, that we have so many
thoroughly successful interiors, which
have been accomplished almost without
aid from professional artists. It is these,
instead of the smaller number of costly
interiors, which give the reputation of
artistic merit to our homes.

Undoubtedly the largest proportion

of successful as well as unsuccessful
domestic art in our country is due to the
efforts of women.   In the great race for
wealth which characterizes our time, it is
demanded that women shall make it
effective by so using it as to distinguish
the family; and nothing distinguishes it
so much as the superiority of the home.
This effort adheres to small as well as
large fortunes, and in fact the necessity
is more pronounced in the case of medi-
ocre than of great ones.   In the former
there is something to be made up—some
protest of worth and ability and intelligence that helps many a home to become
beautiful.

As I have said, a woman feels that
the test of her capacity is that her house
shall not only be comfortable and attractive, but that it shall be arranged
according to the laws of harmony and
beauty.   It is as much the demand of
the hour as that she shall be able to train
her children according to the latest and
most enlightened theories, or that she

shall take part in public and philan-
thropic movements, or understand and
have an opinion on political methods.
These are things which are expected
of every woman who makes a part of
society; and no less is it expected that
her house shall be an appropriate and
beautiful setting for her personality, a
credit to her husband, and an unconscious education for her children.

But it happens that means of education in all of these directions, except
that of decoration, are easily available.
A woman can become a member of a
kindergarten association, and get from
books and study the result of scientific
knowledge of child-life and training.
She can find means to study the ethics of
her relations to her kind and become an
effective philanthropist, or join the league
for political education and acquire a
more or less enlightened understanding of
politics; but who is to formulate for her
the science of beauty, to teach her how
to make the interior aspect of her home

perfect in its adaptation to her circumstances, and as harmonious in colour and
arrangement as a song without words?
She feels that these conditions create a
mental atmosphere serene and yet in-
spiring, and that such surroundings are
as much her birthright and that of her
children as food and clothing of a grade
belonging to their circumstances, but
how is it to be compassed?

Most women ask themselves this
question, and fail to understand that it
is as much of a marvel when a woman
without training or experience creates
a good interior *as a whole*, as if an
amateur in music should compose an
opera. It is not at all impossible for a
woman of good taste—and it must be
remembered that this word means an
educated or cultivated power of selection—to secure harmonious or happily
contrasted colour in a room, and to select
beautiful things in the way of furniture
and belongings; but what is to save her
from the thousand and one mistakes

possible to inexperience in this combination of things which make lasting enjoyment and appropriate perfection in a house? How can she know which rooms will be benefited by sombre or sunny tints, and which exposure will give full sway to her favourite colour or colours? How can she have learned the reliability or want of reliability in certain materials or processes used in decoration, or the rules of treatment which will modify a low and dark room and make it seem light and airy, or "bring down" too high a ceiling and widen narrow walls so as to apparently correct disproportion? These things are the results of laws which she has never studied—laws of compensation and relation, which belong exclusively to the world of colour, and unfortunately they are not so well formulated that they can be committed to memory like rules of grammar; yet all good colour-practice rests upon them as unquestionably as language rests upon grammatical construction.

Of course one may use colour as one can speak a language, purely by imitation and memory, but it is not absolutely reliable practice; and just here comes in the necessity for professional advice.

There are many difficulties in the accomplishment of a perfect house-interior which few householders have had the time or experience to cope with, and yet the fact remains that each mistress of a house believes that unless she vanquishes all difficulties and comes out triumphantly with colours flying at the housetop and enjoyment and admiration following her efforts, she has failed in something which she should have been perfectly able to accomplish. But the obligation is certainly a forced one. It is the result of the modern awakening to the effect of many heretofore unrecognized influences in our lives and the lives and characters of our children. A beautiful home is undoubtedly a great means of education, and of that best

of all education which is unconscious.
To grow up in such a one means a
much more complete and perfect man
or woman than would be possible without that particular influence.

But a perfect home is never created
all at once and by one person, and let
the anxious house-mistress take comfort
in the thought. She should also remember that it is in the nature of beauty
to *grow*, and that a well-rounded and
beautiful family life adds its quota day
by day. Every book, every sketch
or picture—every carefully selected or
characteristic object brought into the
home adds to and makes a part of
a beautiful whole, and no house can
be absolutely perfect without all these
evidences of family life.

It can be made ready for them, com-
pletely and perfectly ready, by professional
skill and knowledge; but if it remained
just where the interior artist or decorator
left it, it would have no more of the
sentiment of domesticity than a statue.

CHAPTER II

CHARACTER IN HOUSES

" For the created still doth shadow forth the mind and will which made it."

" Thou art the very mould of thy creator."

IT NEEDS the combined personality of the family to make the character of the house. No one could say of a house which has family character, "It is one of ——'s houses" (naming one or another successful decorator), because the decorator would have done only what it was his business to do—used technical and artistic knowledge in preparing a proper and correct background for family life. Even in doing that, he must consult family tastes and idiosyncracies if he has the reverence for individuality which belongs to the true artist.

A domestic interior is a thing to which he should give knowledge and not personality, and the puzzled home-

maker, who understands that her world
expects correct use of means of beauty,
as well as character and originality in
her home, need not feel that to secure
the one she must sacrifice the other.

An inexperienced person might think
it an easy thing to make a beautiful
home, because the world is full of
beautiful art and manufactures, and if
there is money to pay for them it
would seem as easy to furnish a house
with everything beautiful as to go out
in the garden and gather beautiful
flowers; but we must remember that
the world is also full of ugly things—
things false in art, in truth and in
beauty—things made to *sell*—made with
only this idea behind them, manufactured on the principle that an artificial fly is made to look something
like a true one in order to catch the
inexpert and the unwary. It is a curious
fact that these false things—manufactures without honesty, without knowledge, without art—have a property of

demoralizing the spirit of the home, and that to make it truly beautiful everything in it must be genuine as well as appropriate, and must also fit into some previously considered scheme of use and beauty.

The esthetic or beautiful aspect of the home, in short, must be created through the mind of the family or owner, and is only maintained by its or his susceptibility to true beauty and appreciation of it. It must, in fact, be a visible mould of invisible matter, like the leaf-mould one finds in mineral springs, which show the wonderful veining, branching, construction and delicacy of outline in a way which one could hardly be conscious of in the actual leaf.

If the grade or dignity of the home requires professional and scholarly art direction, the problem is how to use this professional or artistic advice without delivering over the entire creation into stranger or alien hands; without abdicating the right and privilege of personal expression. If the decorator appreciates this right, his function will be somewhat akin to that of the portrait painter; both are bound to represent the individual or family in their performances, each artist using the truest and best methods of art with the added gift of grace or charm of colour which he possesses, the one giving the physical aspect of his client and the other the mental characteristics, circumstances, position and life of the house-owner and his family. This is the true mission of the decorator, although it is not always so understood. What is called business talent may lead him to invent schemes of costliness which relate far more to his own profit than to the wishes or character of the house-owner.

But it is not always that the assistance of the specialist in decoration and furnishing is necessary. There are many homes where both are quite within the scope of the ordinary man or woman of taste. In fact, the great majority of homes come within these lines, and it is to such home-builders that rules, not involving styles, are especially of use.

The principles of truth and harmony, which underlie all beauty, may be secured in the most inexpensive cottage as well as in the broadest and most imposing residence. Indeed, the cottage has the advantage of that most potent ally of beauty—simplicity—a quality which is apt to be conspicuously absent from the schemes of decoration for the palace.

CHAPTER III

" Mine own hired house."

A LARGE proportion of homes are made in houses which are not owned, but leased, and this prevents each man or family from indicating personal taste in external aspect. A rich man and house-owner may approximate to a true expression of himself even in the outside of his house if he strongly desires it, but a man of moderate means must adapt himself and his family to the house-builder's idea of houses—that is to say, to the idea of the man who has made house-building a trade, and whose experiences have created a form into which houses of moderate cost and fairly universal application may be cast.

Although it is as natural to a man to build or acquire a home as to a bird to build a nest, he has not the same unfettered freedom in construction. He cannot always adapt his house either to the physical or mental size of his family, but must accept what is possible with much the same feeling with which a family of robins might accommodate themselves to a wren's nest, or an oriole to that of a barn-swallow. But the fact remains, that all these accidental homes must, in some way, be brought into harmony with the lives to be lived in them, and the habits and wants of the family; and not only this, they must be made attractive according to the requirements of cultivated society. The effort toward this is instructive, and the pleasure in and enjoyment of the home depends upon the success of the effort. The inmates, as a rule, are quite clear as to what they want to accomplish, but have seldom had sufficient experience to enable them to remedy defects of construction.

There are expedients by which many of the malformations and ugli-nesses of the ordinary "builder's house" may be greatly ameliorated, various small surgical operations which will remedy badly planned rooms, and dispositions of furniture which will restore proportion. We can even, by judicious distribution of planes of colour, apparently lower or raise a ceiling, and widen or lengthen a room, and these expedients, which belong partly to the experience of the deco-rator, are based upon laws which can easily be formulated. Every one can learn something of them by the study of faulty rooms and the enjoyment of satisfactory ones. Indeed, I know no surer or more agreeable way of getting wisdom in the art of decoration than by tracing back sensation to its source, and finding out why certain things are utterly satisfactory, and certain others a positive source of discomfort.

In what are called the "best

houses" we can make our deductions quite as well as in the most faulty, and sometimes get a lesson of avoidance and a warning against law-breaking which will be quite as useful as if it were learned in less than the best.

There is one fault very common in houses which date from a period of some forty or fifty years back, a fault of disproportionate height of ceilings. In a modern house, if one room is large enough to require a lofty ceiling, the architect will manage to make his second floor upon different levels, so as not to inflict the necessary height of large rooms upon narrow halls and small rooms, which should have only a height proportioned to their size. A ten-foot room with a thirteen-foot ceiling makes the narrowness of the room doubly apparent; one feels shut up between two walls which threaten to come together and squeeze one between them, while, on the other hand, a ten-foot room with a nine-foot ceiling may have a really comfortable and cozy effect.

In this case, what is needed is to get rid of the superfluous four feet, and this can be done by cheating the eye into an utter forgetfulness of them. There must be horizontal divisions of colour which attract the attention and make one oblivious of what is above them.

Every one knows the effect of a paper with perpendicular stripes in apparently heightening a ceiling which is too low, but not every one is equally aware of the contrary effect of horizontal lines of varied surface. But in the use of perpendicular lines it is well to remember that, if the room is small, it will appear still smaller if the wall is divided into narrow spaces by vertical lines. If it is large and the ceiling simply low for the size of the room, a good deal can be done by long, simple lines of drapery in curtains and portieres, or in choosing a paper where the composition of design is perpendicular rather than diagonal.

To apparently lower a high ceiling in a small room, the wall should be treated horizontally in different materials. Three feet of the base can be covered with coarse canvas or buckram and finished with a small wood moulding. Six feet of plain wall above this, painted the same shade as the canvas, makes the space of which the eye is most aware. This space should be finished with a picture moulding, and the four superfluous feet of wall above it must be treated as a part of the ceiling. The cream-white of the actual ceiling should be brought down on the side walls for a space of two feet, and this has the effect of apparently enlarging the room, since the added mass of light tint seems to broaden it. There still remain two feet of space between the picture moulding and ceiling-line which may be treated as a *ceiling-border* in inconspicuous design upon the same cream ground, the design to be in darker, but of the same tint as the ceiling.

The floor in such a room as this should either be entirely covered with plain carpeting, or, if it has rugs at all, there should be several, as one single rug, not entirely covering the floor, would have the effect of confining the apparent size of the room to the actual size of the rug.

If the doors and windows in such a room are high and narrow, they can be made to come into the scheme by placing the curtain and portiere rods below the actual height and covering the upper space with thin material, either full or plain, of the same colour as the upper wall. A brocaded muslin, stained or dyed to match the wall, answers this purpose admirably, and is really better in its place than the usual expedient of stained glass or open-work wood transom. A good expedient is to have the design already carried around the wall painted in the same colour upon a piece of stretched muslin. This is simple but effective treatment, and is an instance of the kind of thought or knowledge that must be used in remedying faults of construction.

Colour has much to do with the apparent size of rooms, a room in light tints always appearing to be larger than a deeply coloured one.

Perhaps the most difficult problem in adaptation is the high, narrow city house, built and decorated by the block by the builder, who is also a speculator in real estate, and whose activity was chiefly exercised before the ingenious devices of the modern architect were known. These houses exist in quantities in our larger and older cities, and mere slices of space as they are, are the theatres where the home-life of many refined and beauty-loving intelligences must be played.

In such houses as these, the task of fitting them to the cultivated eyes and somewhat critical tests of modern society generally falls to the women who represent the family, and calls for an amount of ability which would serve to build any number of creditable houses ; yet this is constantly being done and well done for not one, but many families.   I know one such, which is quite a model of a charming city home and yet was evolved from one of the worst of its kind and period. In this case the family had fallen heir to the house and were therefore justified in the one radical change which metamorphosed the entrance - hall, from a long, narrow passage, with an apparently interminable stairway occupying half its width, to a small reception-hall seemingly enlarged by a

HALL IN CITY HOUSE SHOWING EFFECT OF STAIRCASE DIVIDED AND TURNED TO REAR

judicious placing of the mirrors which had formerly been a part of the " fixtures " of the parlour and dining-room.

The reception-room was accomplished by cutting off the lower half of the staircase, which had extended itself to within three feet of the front door, and turning it directly around, so that it ends at the back instead of the front of the hall. The two cut ends are connected by a platform, thrown across from wall to wall, and furnished with a low railing of carved panels, and turned spindles, which gives a charming balcony effect. The passage to the back hall and stairs passes under the balcony and upper end of the staircase, while the space under the lower stair-end, screened by a portière, adds a coat-closet to the conveniences of the reception-hall.

This change was not a difficult thing to accomplish, it was simply an *expedient*, but it has the value of care-

fully planned construction, and reminds one of the clever utterance of
the immortal painter who said, " I
never lose an accident."

Indeed the ingenious home-maker
often finds that the worse a thing is,
the better it can be made by competent and careful study. To complete and adapt incompetent things
to orderliness and beauty, to harmonise incongruous things into a
perfect whole requires and exercises
ability of a high order, and the consciousness of its possession is no small
satisfaction.   That it is constantly
being done shows how much real
cleverness is necessary to ordinary
life—and reminds one of the patri-
otic New York state senator who de-
clared that it required more ability
to cross Broadway safely at high tide,
than to be a great statesman.   And
truly, to make a good house out of
a poor one, or a beautiful interior

from an ugly one, requires far more thought, and far more original talent, than to decorate an important new one. The one follows a travelled path—the other makes it.

Of course competent knowledge saves one from many difficulties; and faults of construction must be met by knowledge, yet this is often greatly aided by natural cleverness, and in the course of long practice in the decorative arts, I have seen such refreshing and charming results from thoughtful untrained intelligence,—I might almost say inspiration,—that I have great respect for its manifestations; especially when exercised in un-authoritative fashion.

CHAPTER IV

COLOUR IN HOUSES

" Heaven gives us of its colour, for our joy,
Hues which have words and speak to ye of heaven."

ALTHOUGH the very existence of a house is a matter of construction, its general interior effect is almost entirely the result of colour treatment and careful and cultivated selection of accessories.

Colour in the house includes much that means furniture, in the way of carpets, draperies, and all the modern conveniences of civilization, but as it precedes and dictates the variety of all these things from the authoritative standpoint of wall treatment, it is well to study its laws and try to reap the full benefit of its influence.

As far as effect is concerned, the colour of a room creates its atmosphere. It may be cheerful or sad, cosy or repellent according to its quality or force. Without colour it is only a bare canvas, which might, but does not picture our lives.

We understand many of the properties of colour, and have unconsciously learned some of its laws;—but what may be called the *science* of colour has never been formulated. So far as we understand it, its principles correspond curiously to those of melodious sound. It is as impossible to produce the best effect from one tone or colour, as to make a melody upon one note of the harmonic scale; it is skilful *variation* of tone, the gradation or even judicious opposition of tint which gives exquisite satisfaction to the eye. In music, sequence produces this effect upon the ear, and in colour, juxtaposition and gradation upon the eye. Notes follow notes in melody as shade follows shade in colour. We find no need of even dif-

ferent names for the qualities peculiar
to the two; scale—notes—tones—
harmonies—the words express effects
common to colour as well as to music,
but colour has this advantage, that its
harmonies can be *fixed*, they do not
die with the passing moment; once
expressed they remain as a constant
and ever-present delight.

Notes of the sound-octave have
been gathered by the musicians from
widely different substances, and carefully linked in order and sequence to
make a harmonious scale which may
be learned; but the painter, conscious of colour-harmonies, has as yet
no written law by which he can produce them.

The " born colourist " is one who
without special training, or perhaps in
spite of it, can unerringly combine or
oppose tints into compositions which
charm the eye and satisfy the sense.
Even among painters it is by no means

a common gift. It is almost more
rare to find a picture distinguished for
its harmony and beauty of colour, than
to see a room in which nothing jars
and everything works together for
beauty. It seems strange that this
should be a rarer personal gift than the
musical sense, since nature apparently
is far more lavish of her lessons for
the eye than for the ear; and it is
curious that colour, which at first sight
seems a more apparent and simple
fact than music, has not yet been
written. Undoubtedly there is a colour scale, which has its sharps and
flats, its high notes and low notes, its
chords and discords, and it is not impossible that in the future science may
make it a means of regulated and
written harmonies :——that some master colourist who has mechanical and
inventive genius as well, may so arrange them that they can be played
by rule; that colour may have its

Mozart or Beethoven—its classic melodies, its familiar tunes. The mu-
sician, as I have said—has gathered
his tones from every audible thing in
nature—and fitted and assorted and
built them into a science ; and why
should not some painter who is also a
scientist take the many variations of
colour which lie open to his sight,
and range and fit and combine, and
write the formula, so that a child may
read it ?

We already know enough to be
very sure that the art is founded upon
laws, although they are not thoroughly understood. Principles of masses,
spaces, and gradations underlie all accidental harmonies of colour;—just as
in music, the simple, strong, under-
chords of the bass must be the ground
for all the changes and trippings of
the upper melodies.

It is easy, if one studies the subject,
to see how the very likeness of these

two esthetic forces illustrate the laws
of each,—in the principles of relation,
gradation, and scale.

Until very recently the relation of
colour to the beauty of a house interior was quite unrecognised. If it
existed in any degree of perfection
it was an accident, a result of the
softening and beautifying effect of
time, or of harmonious human living.
Where it existed, it was felt as a mys-
terious charm belonging to the home ;
something which pervaded it, but had
no separate being ; an attractive ghost
which attached itself to certain houses,
followed certain people, came by
chance, and was a mystery which no
one understood, but every one acknowledged. Now we know that
this something which distinguished
particular rooms, and made beautiful
particular houses, was a definite result
of laws of colour accidentally applied.

To avail ourselves of this influence upon the moods and experiences of life is to use a power positive in its effects as any spiritual or intellectual influence. It gives the kind of joy we find in nature, in the golden-green of light under tree-branches, or the mingled green and gray of tree and rock shadows, or the pearl and rose of sunrise and sunset. We call the deep content which results from such surroundings the influence of nature, and forget to name the less spiritual, the more human condition of well-being which comes to us in our homes from being surrounded with something which in a degree atones for lack of nature's beauty.

It is a different well-being, and lacks the full tide of electric enjoyment which comes from living for the hour under the sky and in the breadths of space, but it atones by substituting something of our own invention, which surprises us by its compensations, and confounds us by its power.

CHAPTER V

THE LAW OF APPROPRIATENESS

I HAVE laid much stress upon the value of colour in interior decoration, but to complete the beauty of the home something more than happy choice of tints is required. It needs careful and educated selection of furniture and fittings, and money enough to indulge in the purchase of an intrinsically good thing instead of a medium one. It means even something more than the love of beauty and cultivation of it, and that is a perfect adherence to the *law of appropriateness*.

This is, after all, the most important quality of every kind of decoration, the one binding and general condition of its accomplishment. It requires such a careful fitting together of all the means of beauty as to leave no part of the house, whatever may be its use, without the same care for appropriate completeness which goes to the more apparent features. The cellar, the kitchen, the closets, the servants' bedrooms must all share in the thought which makes the genuinely beautiful home and the genuinely perfect life. It must be possible to go from the top to the bottom of the house, finding everywhere agreeable, suitable, and thoughtful furnishings. The beautiful house must consider the family as a whole, and not make a museum of rare and costly things in the drawing-room, the library, the dining-room and family bedrooms, leaving that important part of the whole machinery, the service, untouched by the spirit of beauty. The same care in choice of colour will be as well bestowed on the servants' floor as on those devoted to the

family, and curtains, carpets and furniture may possess as much beauty and
yet be perfectly appropriate to servants' use.

On this upper floor, it goes almost
without saying, that the walls must be
painted in oil-colour instead of covered with paper. That the floors
should be uncarpeted except for bedside rugs which are easily removable.
That bedsteads should be of iron, the
mattress with changeable covers, the
furniture of painted and enameled instead of polished wood, and in short
the conditions of healthful cleanliness
as carefully provided as if the rooms
were in a hospital instead of a private house—but the added comfort
of carefully chosen wall colour, and
bright, harmonizing, washable chintz
in curtains and bed-covers.

These things have an influence upon the spirit of the home; they are
a part of its spiritual beauty, giving a

satisfied and approving consciousness
to the home-makers, and a sense of
happiness in the service of the family.

In the average, or small house,
there is room for much improvement
in the treatment and furnishing of
servants' bedrooms; and this is not
always from indifference, but because
they are out of daily sight, and also
from a belief that it would add seri-
ously to the burden of housekeeping
to see that they are kept up to the
standard of family sleeping-rooms.

In point of fact, however, good
surroundings are potent civilizers, and
a house-servant whose room is well
and carefully furnished feels an added
value in herself, which makes her treat
herself respectfully in the care of her
room.

If it pleases her, the training she
receives in the care of family rooms
will be reflected in her own, and
painstaking arrangements made for

her pleasure will perhaps be recognised as an obligation.

Of course the fact must be recognised, that the occupant is not always a permanent one; that it may at times be a fresh importation directly from a city tenement; therefore, everything in the room should be able to sustain very radical treatment in the way of scrubbing and cleaning. Wall papers, unwashable rugs and curtains are out of the question; yet even with these limitations it is possible to make a charming and reasonably inexpensive room, which would be attractive to cultivated as well as uncultivated taste. It is in truth mostly a matter of colour; of coloured walls, and harmonising furniture and draperies, which are in themselves well adapted to their place.

As I have said elsewhere, the walls in a servant's bedroom—and preferably in any sleeping-room—should for sanitary reasons be painted in oil colours, but the possibilities of decorative treatment in this medium are by no means limited. All of the lighter shades of green, blue, yellow, and rose are as permanent, and as easily cleaned, as the dull grays and drabs and mud-colours which are often used upon bedroom walls—especially those upper ones which are above the zone of ornament, apparently under the impression that there is virtue in their very ugliness.

" A good clean gray " some worthy housewife will instruct the painter to use, and the result will be a dead mixture of various lively and pleasant tints, any one of which might be charming if used separately, or modified with white. A small room with walls of a very light spring green, or a pale turquoise blue, or white with the dash of vermilion and touch of yellow ochre which produces salmon-

pink, is quite as durably and service-
ably coloured as if it were chocolate-
brown, or heavy lead-colour; indeed
its effect upon the mind is like a spring
day full of sunshine instead of one
dark with clouds or lowering storms.

The rule given elsewhere for colour
in light or dark exposure will hold
good for service bedrooms as well as
for the important rooms of the house.
That is; if a bedroom for servants' use
is on the north or shadowed side of
the house, let the colour be salmon
or rose pink, cream white, or spring
green; but if it is on the sunny side,
the tint should be turquoise, or pale
blue, or a grayish-green, like the green
of a field of rye. With such walls, a
white iron bedstead, enameled furniture, curtains of white, or a flowered
chintz which repeats or contrasts with
the colour of the walls, bedside and
bureau rugs of the tufted cotton which
is washable, or of the new rag-rugs of

which the colours are "water fast," the room is absolutely good, and can be used as an influence upon a lower or higher intelligence.

As a matter of utility the toilet service should be always of white; so that there will be no chance for the slovenly mismatching which results from breakage of any one of the different pieces, when of different colours. A handleless or mis-matched pitcher will change the entire character of a room and should never be tolerated.

If the size of the room will warrant it, a rocking-chair or easy-chair should always be part of its equipment, and the mattress and bed-springs should be of a quality to give ease to tired bones, for these things have to do with the spirit of the house.

It may be said that the colouring and furnishing of the servants' bedroom is hardly a part of house

decoration, but in truth house decoration at its best is a means of happiness, and no householder can achieve
permanent happiness without making
the service of the family sharers in it.

What I have said with regard to
painted walls in plain tints applies to
bedrooms of every grade, but where
something more than merely agreeable colour effect is desired a stencilled decoration from the simplest
to the most elaborate can be added.
There are many ways of using this
method, some of which partake very
largely of artistic effect; indeed a
thoroughly good stencil pattern may
reproduce the best instances of design,
and in the hands of a skilful work-
man who knows how to graduate and
vary contrasting or harmonising tints
it becomes a very artistic method and
deserves a place of high honour in the
art of decoration.

Its simplest form is that of a sten-

1, AND 2, STENCILED BORDERS FOR BATH-ROOM DECORATION; 3, 4 AND 5, STENCILED
BORDERS FOR HALLS (BY DUNHAM WHEELER)

cilled border in flat tints used either
in place of a cornice or as the border of a wall-paper is used. This, of
course, is a purely mechanical per-
formance, and one with which every
house-painter is familiar. After this
we come to borders of repeating design used as friezes. This can be done
with the most delicate and delightful
effect, although the finished wall will
still be capable of withstanding
the most energetic annual scrubbing.
Frieze borders of this kind starting
with strongly contrasting colour at
the top and carried downward through
gradually fading tints until they are
lost in the general colour of the wall
have an openwork grille effect which
is very light and graceful. There are
infinite possibilities in the use of stencil design without counting the introduction of gold and silver, and bronzes
of various iridescent hues which are
more suitable for rooms of general

use than for bedrooms. Indeed in
sleeping-rooms the use of metallic
colour is objectionable because it will
not stand washing and cleaning without defacement. The ideal bedroom
is one that if the furniture were removed a stream of water from a hose
might be played upon its walls and
ceiling without injury. I always remember with pleasure a pink and
silver room belonging to a young girl,
where the salmon-pink walls were
deepened in colour at the top into
almost a tint of vermilion which had
in it a trace of green. It was, in fact,
an addition of spring green dropped
into the vermilion and carelessly
stirred, so that it should be mixed but
not incorporated. Over this shaded
and mixed colour for the space of
three feet was stencilled a fountain-
like pattern in cream-white, the arches
of the pattern filled in with almost a
lace-work of design. The whole up-

per part had an effect like carved alabaster and was indescribably light and graceful.

The bed and curtain-rods of silver-lacquer, and the abundant silver of the dressing-table gave a frosty contrast which was necessary in a room of so warm a general tone. This is an example of very delicate and truly artistic treatment of stencil-work, and one can easily see how it can be used either in simple or elaborate fashion with great effect.

Irregularly placed floating forms of Persian or Arabic design are often admirably stencilled in colour upon a painted wall; but in this case the colours should be varied and not too strong. A group of forms floating away from a window-frame or cornice can be done in two shades of the wall colour, one of which is positively darker and one lighter than the ground. If to these two shades some delicately contrasting colour is occasionally added the effect is not only pleasing, but belongs to a thoroughly good style.

One seldom tires of a good stencilled wall; probably because it is intrinsic, and not applied in the sense of paper or textiles. It carries an air of permanency which discourages change or experiment, but it requires considerable experience in decoration to execute it worthily; and not only this, there should be a strong feeling for colour and taste and education in the selection of design, for though the form of the stencilled pattern may be graceful, and gracefully combined, it must always—to be permanently satisfactory—have a geometrical basis. It is somewhat difficult to account for the fact that what we call natural forms, of plants and flowers, which are certainly beautiful and graceful in themselves, and grow into shapes which

delight us with their freedom and
beauty, do not give the best satisfaction as motives for interior decoration.
Construction in the architectural sense
—the strength and squareness of
walls, ceilings, and floors—seem to re-
ject the yielding character of design
founded upon natural forms, and demand something which answers more
sympathetically to their own qualities.
Perhaps it is for this reason that we
find the grouping and arrangement
of horizontal and perpendicular lines
and blocks in the old Greek borders
so everlastingly satisfactory.

It is the principle or requirement,
of geometric base in interior design
which, coupled with our natural delight in yielding or growing forms,
has maintained through all the long
history of decoration what is called
conventionalised flower design.   We
find this in every form or method of
decorative art, from embroidery to

sculpture, from the Lotus of Egypt to the Rose of England, and although it results in a sort of crucifixion of the natural beauty of the flower, in the hands of great designers it has become an authoritative style of art.

Of course, there are flower-forms which are naturally geometric, which have conventionalised themselves. Many of the intricate Moorish frets and Indian carvings are literal translations of flower-forms geometrically repeated, and here they lend themselves so perfectly to the decoration of even exterior walls that the fretted arches of some Eastern buildings seem almost to have grown of themselves, with all their elaboration, into the world of nature and art.

The separate flowers of the gracefully tossing lilac plumes, and the five- and six-leaved flowers of the pink, have become in this way a very part of the everlasting walls, as the acanthus leaf has become the marble blossom of thousands of indestructible columns.

These are the classics of design and hold the same relation to ornament printed on paper and silk that we find in the music of the Psalms, as compared with the tinkle of the ballad.

There are other methods of decoration in oils which will meet the wants of the many who like to exercise their own artistic feelings and ability in their houses or rooms. The painting of flower-friezes upon canvas which can afterward be mounted upon the wall is a never-ending source of pleasure; and many of these friezes have a charm and intimacy which no merely professional painter can rival. These are especially suitable for bedrooms, since there they may be as personal as the inmate pleases without undue unveiling of thoughts, fancies,

or personal experiences to the public.
A favourite flower or a favourite motto
or selection may be the motive of a
charming decoration, if the artist has
sufficient art-knowledge to subordi-
nate it to its architectural juxtaposition.   A narrow border of fixed repeating forms like a rug-border will
often fulfil the necessity for architectural lines, and confine the flower-
border into limits which justify its
freedom of composition.

If one wishes to mount a favourite
motto or quotation on the walls,
where it may give constant suggestion
or pleasure——or even be a help to
thoughtful and conscientious living——
there can be no better fashion than
the style of the old illuminated mis-
sals.   Dining - rooms and chimney-
pieces are often very appropriately
decorated in this way ; the words
running on scrolls which are half un-
rolled and half hidden, and showing

a conventionalised background of fruit and flowers.

In all these things the *knowingness*, which is the result of study, tells very strongly—and it is quite worth while to give a good deal of study to the subject of this kind of decoration before expending the requisite amount of work upon a painted frieze.

Canvas friezes have the excellent merit of being not only durable and cleanable, but they belong to the category of pictures; to what Ruskin calls "portable art," and one need not grudge the devotion of considerable time, study, and effort to their doing, since they are really detachable property, and can be removed from one house or room and carried to another at the owner's or artist's will.

There is room for the exercise of much artistic ability in this direction, as the fact of being able to paint the decoration in parts and afterward

place it, makes it possible for an
amateur to do much for the enhance-
ment of her own house.

More than any other room in the
house, the bedroom will show personal character.   Even when it is not
planned for particular occupation, the
characteristics of the inmate will write
themselves unmistakably in the room.
If the college boy is put in the white
and gold bedroom for even a vacation
period, there will shortly come into
its atmosphere an element of sporting
and out-of-door life.   Banners and
balls and bats, and emblems of the
" wild thyme " order will colour its
whiteness; and life of the growing
kind make itself felt in the midst
of sanctity.   In the same way, girls
would change the bare asceticism of a
monk's cell into a bower of lilies and
roses; a fit place for youth and un-
praying innocence.

The bedrooms of a house are a

pretty sure test of the liberality of mind and understanding of character of the mother or house-ruler. As each room is in a certain sense the home of the individual occupant, almost the shell of his or her mind, there will be something narrow and despotic in the house-rules if this is not allowed. Yet, even individuality of taste and expression must scrupulously follow sanitary laws in the furnishing of the bedroom. " Stuffy things " of any sort should be avoided. The study should be to make it beautiful without such things, and a liberal use of washable textiles in curtains, portières, bed and table covers, will give quite as much sense of luxury as heavily papered walls and costly upholstery. In fact, one may run through all the variations from the daintiest and most befrilled and elegant of guests' bedrooms, to the " boys' room," which includes all or any of the various implements of sport or the hobbies of the boy collector, and yet keep inviolate the principles of harmony, colour, and appropriateness to use, and so accomplish beauty.

The absolute ruling of light, air, and cleanliness are quite compatible with individual expression.

It is this characteristic aspect of the different rooms which makes up the beauty of the house as a whole. If the purpose of each is left to develop itself through good conditions, the whole will make that most delightful of earthly things, a beautiful home.

CHAPTER VI

KITCHENS

THE kitchen is an important part of the perfect house and should be a recognised sharer in its quality of beauty; not alone the beauty which consists of a successful adaptation of means to ends, but the kind which is independently and positively attractive to the eye.

In costly houses it is not hard to attain this quality or the rarer one of a union of beauty, with perfect adaptation to use; but where it must be reached by comparatively inexpensive methods, the difficulty is greater.

Tiled walls, impervious to moisture, and repellent of fumes, are ideal boundaries of a kitchen, and may be beautiful in colour, as well as virtuous in conduct. They may even be

laid with gradations of alluring mineral tints, but, of course, this is out of
the question in cheap buildings; and
in demonstrating the possibility of
beauty and intrinsic merit in small and
comparatively inexpensive houses, tiles
and marbles must be ruled out of the
scheme of kitchen perfection. Plaster, painted in agreeable tints of oil
colour is commendable, but one can
do better by covering the walls with
the highly enamelled oil-cloth commonly used for kitchen tables and
shelves. This material is quite mar-
vellous in its combination of use and
effect. Its possibilities were discovered
by a young housewife whose small
kitchen formed part of a city apartment, and whose practical sense was
joined to a discursive imagination.
After this achievement—which she
herself did not recognise as a stroke of
genius—she added a narrow shelf running entirely around the room, which

carried a decorative row of blue willow-pattern plates. A dresser, hung with a graduated assortment of blue enamelled sauce-pans, and other kitchen implements of the same enticing ware, a floor covered with the heaviest of oil-cloth, laid in small diamond-shapes of blue, between blocks of white, like a mosaic pavement, were the features of a kitchen which was, and is, after several years of strenuous wear, a joy to behold. It was from the first, not only a delight to the clever young housewife and her friends, but it performed the miracle of changing the average servant into a careful and excellent one, zealous for the cleanliness and perfection of her small domain, and performing her kitchen functions with unexampled neatness.

The mistress—who had standards of perfection in all things, whether great or small, and was moreover of Southern blood—confessed that her

ideal of service in her glittering kitch-
en was not a clever red-haired Hiber-
nian, but a slim mulatto, wearing a
snow-white turban ; and this long-
ing seemed so reasonable, and so im-
pressed my fancy, that whenever I
think of the shining blue-and-silver
kitchen, I seem to see within it the
graceful sway of figure and coffee-
coloured face which belongs to the
half-breed African race, certain rare
specimens of which are the most beautiful of domestic adjuncts.

I have used this expedient of oil-
cloth-covered walls——for which I am
anxious to give the inventor due credit
——in many kitchens, and certain bath-
rooms, and always with success.

It must be applied as if it were
wall-paper, except that, as it is a heavy
material, the paste must be thicker.
It is also well to have in it a small
proportion of carbolic acid, both as a
disinfectant and a deterrent to paste-

loving mice, or any other household pest. The cloth must be carefully fitted into corners, and whatever shelving or wood fittings are used in the room, must be placed against it, after it is applied, instead of having the cloth cut and fitted around them.

When well mounted, it makes a solid, porcelain-like wall, to which dust and dirt will not easily adhere, and which can be as easily and effectually cleaned as if it were really porcelain or marble.

Such wall treatment will go far toward making a beautiful kitchen. Add to this a well-arranged dresser for blue or white kitchen china, with a closed cabinet for the heavy iron utensils which can hardly be included in any scheme of kitchen beauty; curtained cupboards and short window-hangings of blue, or "Turkey red"—which are invaluable for colour, and always washable; a painted floor

—which is far better than oil-cloth,
and one has the elements of a satisfactory scheme of beauty.

A French kitchen, with its white-
washed walls, its shining range and
rows upon rows of gleaming copper-
ware, is an attractive subject for a
painter; and there is no reason why
an American kitchen, in a house distinguished for beauty in all its family
and semi-public rooms, should not
also be beautiful in the rooms devoted to service. We can if we will
make much even in a decorative way
of our enamelled and aluminum kitch-
en-ware; we may hang it in graduated
rows over the chimney-space—as the
French cook parades her coppers—
and arrange these necessary things
with an eye to effect, while we secure
perfect convenience of use. They
are all pleasant of aspect if care and
thought are devoted to their arrangement, and it is really of quite as

much value to the family to have a
charming and perfectly appointed
kitchen, as to possess a beautiful and
comfortable parlour or sitting-room,

Every detail should be considered
from the double point of view of use
and effect. If the curtains answer
the two purposes of shading sunlight,
or securing privacy at night, and of
giving pleasing colour and contrast to
the general tone of the interior, they
perform a double function, each of
of which is valuable.

If the chairs are chosen for strength
and use, and are painted or stained to
match the colour of the floor, they add
to the satisfaction of the eye, as well
as minister to the house service. A
pursuance of this thought adds to the
harmony of the house both in aspect
and actual beauty of living. Of
course in selecting such furnishings of
the kitchen as chairs, one must bear
in mind that even their legitimate

use may include standing, as well as sitting upon them; that they may be made temporary resting-places for scrubbing pails, brushes, and other cleaning necessities, and therefore they must be made of painted wood; but this should not discourage the provision of a cane-seated rocking-chair for each servant, as a comfort for weary bones when the day's work is over.

In establishments which include a servants' dining- or sitting-room, these moderate luxuries are a thing of course, but in houses where at most but two maids are employed they are not always considered, although they certainly should be.

If a corner can be appropriated to evening leisure—where there is room for a small, brightly covered table, a lamp, a couple of rocking-chairs, work-baskets and a book or magazine, it answers in a small way to the family evening-room, where all gather for rest and comfort.

There is no reason why the wall space above it should not have its cabinet for photographs and the usually cherished prayer-book which maids love both to possess and display. Such possessions answer exactly to the *bric-a-brac* of the drawing-room; ministering to the same human instinct in its primitive form, and to the inherent enjoyment of the beautiful which is the line of demarcation between the tribes of animals and those of men.

If one can use this distinctly human trait as a lever to raise crude humanity into the higher region of the virtues, it is certainly worth while to consider pots and pans from the point of view of their decorative ability.

CHAPTER VII

COLOUR WITH REFERENCE TO LIGHT

IN choosing colour for walls and ceilings, it is most necessary to consider the special laws which govern its application to house interiors.

The tint of any particular room should be chosen not only with reference to personal liking, but first of all, to the quantity and quality of light which pervades it. A north room will require warm and bright treatment, warm reds and golden browns, or pure gold colours. Gold-colour used in sash curtains will give an effect of perfect sunshine in a dark and shadowy room, but the same treatment in a room fronting the south would produce an almost insupportable brightness.

I will illustrate the modifications

made necessary in tint by different exposure to light, by supposing that some one member of the family prefers yellow to all other colours, one who has enough of the chameleon in her nature to feel an instinct to bask in sunshine. I will also suppose that the room most conveniently devoted to the occupation of this member has a southern exposure. If yellow must be used in her room, the quality of it should be very different from that which could be properly and profitably used in a room with a northern exposure, and it should differ not only in intensity, but actually in tint. If it is necessary, on account of personal preference, to use yellow in a sunny room, it should be lemon, instead of ochre or gold-coloured yellow, because the latter would repeat, sunlight. There are certain shades of yellow, where white has been largely used in the mixture, which are capable of greenish reflections. This is where the white is of so pure a quality as to suggest blue, and consequently under the influence of yellow to suggest green. We often find yellow dyes in silks the shadows of which are positive fawn colour or even green, instead of orange as we might expect; still, even with modifications, yellow should properly be reserved for sunless rooms, where it acts the part almost of the blessed sun itself in giving cheerfulness and light. Going from a sun-lighted atmosphere, or out of actual sunlight into a yellow room, one would miss the sense of shelter which is so grateful to eyes and senses a little dazzled by the brilliance of out-of-door lights; whereas a room darkened or shaded by a piazza, or somewhat chilled by a northern exposure and want of sun, would be warmed and comforted by tints of gold-coloured yellow.

Interiors with a southern exposure should be treated with cool, light colours, blues in various shades, water-greens, and silvery tones which will contrast with the positive yellow of sunlight.

It is by no means a merely arbitrary rule. Colours are actually warm or cold in temperature, as well as in effect upon the eye or the imagination, in fact the words cover a long-tested fact. I remember being told by a painter of his placing a red sunset landscape upon the flat roof of a studio building to dry, and on going to it a few hours afterward he found the surface of it so warm to the touch —so sensibly warmer than the gray and blue and green pictures around it—that he brought a thermometer to test it, and found it had acquired and retained heat. It was actually warmer by degrees than the gray and blue pictures in the same sun exposure.

We instinctively wear warm colours in winter and dispense with them in summer, and this simple fact may explain the art which allots what we call warm colour to rooms without sun. When we say warm colours, we mean yellows, reds with all their gradations, gold or sun browns, and dark browns and black. When we say cool colours—whites, blues, grays, and cold greens—for greens may be warm or cold, according to their composition or intensity. A water-green is a cold colour, so is a pure emerald green, so also a blue-green; while an olive, or a gold-green comes into the category of warm colours. This is because it is a composite colour made of a union of warm and cold colours; the brown and yellow in its composition being in excess of the blue; as pink also, which is a mixture of red and white; and lavender, which is a mixture of red, white, and blue, stand as intermediate between two extremes.

Having duly considered the effect of light upon colour, we may fearlessly choose tints for every room according to personal preferences or tastes. If we like one warm colour better than another, there is no reason why that one should not predominate in every room in the house which has a shadow exposure. If we like a cold colour it should be used in many of the sunny rooms.

I believe we do not give enough importance to this matter of personal liking in tints. We select our friends from sympathy. As a rule, we do not philosophise much about it, although we may recognise certain principles in our liking; it is those to whom our hearts naturally open that we invite in and have joy in their companionship, and we might surely follow our likings in the matter of colour, as well as in friendship, and thereby add much to our happiness. Curiously enough we often speak of the colour of a mind—and I once knew a child who persisted in calling people by the names of colours; not the colour of their clothes, but some mind-tint which he felt. "The blue lady" was his especial favourite, and I have no doubt the presence or absence of that particular colour made a difference in his content all the days of his life.

The colour one likes is better for tranquillity and enjoyment—more conducive to health; and exercises an actual living influence upon moods. For this reason, if no other, the colour of a room should never be arbitrarily prescribed or settled for the one who is to be its occupant. It should be as much a matter of *nature* as the lining of a shell is to the mussel, or as the colour of the wings of a butterfly.

In fact the mind which we cannot see may have a colour of its own, and it is natural that it should choose to dwell within its own influence.

We do not know *why* we like certain colours, but we do, and let that suffice, and let us live with them, as gratefully as we should for more explainable ministry.

If colours which we like have a soothing effect upon us, those which we do not like are, on the other hand, an unwelcome influence. If a woman says in her heart, I hate green, or red, or I dislike any one colour, and then is obliged to live in its neighbourhood, she will find herself dwelling with an enemy. We all know that there are colours of which a little is enjoyable when a mass would be unendurable. Predominant scarlet would be like close companionship with a brass band, but a note of scarlet is one of the most valuable of sensations. The gray compounded of black and white would be a wet blanket to all bubble of wit or spring of fancy, but the shadows of rose colour are gray, pink-tinted it is true; indeed the shadow of pink used to be known by the name of *ashes of roses*. I remember seeing once in Paris—that home of bad general decoration—a room in royal purples; purple velvet on walls, furniture, and hangings. One golden Rembrandt in the middle of a long wall, and a great expanse of ochre-coloured par-quetted floor were all that saved it from the suggestion of a royal tomb. As it was, I left the apartment with a feeling of treading softly as when we pass through a door hung with crape. Vagaries of this kind are remediable when they occur in cravats, or bon-nets, or gloves—but a room in the wrong colour! Saints and the angels preserve us!

SITTING-ROOM IN "WILD WOOD," ONTEORA (BELONGING TO MISS LUISITA LELAND)

The number, size, and placing of
the windows will greatly affect the
intensity of colour to be used. It
must always be remembered that any
interior is dark as compared with out-
of-doors, and that in the lightest
room there will be dark corners or
spaces where the colour chosen as
chief tint will seem much darker than
it really is. A paper or textile chos-
en in a good light will look several
shades darker when placed in large
unbroken masses or spaces upon the
wall, and a fully furnished room will
generally be much darker when com-
pleted than might be expected in
planning it. For this reason, in
choosing a favourite tint, it is better
on many accounts to choose it in as
light a shade as one finds agreeable.
It can be repeated in stronger tones
in furniture or in small and unimportant furnishings of the room, but
the wall tone should never be deeper

than medium in strength, at the risk of having all the light absorbed by the colour, and of losing a sense of atmosphere in the room. There is another reason for this, which is that many colours are agreeable, even to their lovers, only in light tones. The moment they get below medium they become insistent, and make themselves of too much importance. In truth colour has qualities which are almost personal, and is well worth studying in all its peculiarities, because of its power to affect our happiness.

The principles of proper use of colour in house interiors are not difficult to master. It is unthinking, unreflective action which makes so many unrestful interiors of homes. The creator of a home should consider, in the first place, that it is a matter as important as climate, and as difficult to get away from, and that the first shades of colour used in a room upon walls or ceiling, must govern everything else that enters in the way of furnishing; that the colour of walls prescribes that which must be used in floors, curtains, and furniture. Not that these must necessarily be of the same tint as walls, but that wall-tints must govern the choice.

All this makes it necessary to take first steps carefully, to select for each room the colour which will best suit the taste, feeling, or bias of the occupant, always considering the exposure of the room and the use of it.

After the relation of colour to light is established—with personal preferences duly taken into account —the next law is that of gradation. The strongest, and generally the purest, tones of colour belong naturally at the base, and the floor of a room means the base upon which the scheme of decoration is to be built.

The carpet, or floor covering, should carry the strongest tones.   If a single tint is to be used, the walls must take the next gradation, and the ceiling the last.   These gradations must be far enough removed from each other in depth of tone to be quite apparent, but not to lose their relation.   The connecting grades may appear in furniture covering and draperies, thus giving different values in the same tone, the relation between them being perfectly apparent.   These three masses of related colour are the groundwork upon which one can play infinite variations, and is really the same law upon which a picture is composed. There are foreground, middle-distance, and sky—and in a properly coloured room, the floors, walls, and ceiling bear the same relation to each other as the grades of colour in a picture, or in a landscape.

Fortunately we keep to this **law**

almost by instinct, and yet I have
seen a white-carpeted floor in a room
with a painted ceiling of considerable
depth of colour.   Imagine the effect
where this rule of gradation or as-
cending scale is reversed.   A tinted
floor of cream colour, or even white,
and a ceiling as deep in colour as a
landscape.   One feels as if they themselves were reversed, and standing
upon their heads.   Certainly if we
ignore this law we lose our sense of
base or foundation, and although
we may not know exactly why, we
shall miss the restfulness of a properly constructed scheme of decoration.

The rule of gradation includes
also that of massing of colour.   In all
simple treatment of interiors, whatever colour is chosen should be allowed space enough to establish its
influence, broadly and freely, and
here again we get a lesson from nat-

ure in the massing of colour. It
should not be broken into patches
and neutralised by divisions, but used
in large enough spaces to dominate,
or bring into itself or its own influence all that is placed in the room.
If this rule is disregarded every piece
of furniture unrelated to the whole
becomes a spot, it has no real connection with the room, and the room
itself, instead of a harmonious and
delightful influence, akin to that of
a sun-flushed dawn or a sunset sky,
is like a picture where there is no
composition, or a book where inci-
dent is jumbled together without relation to the story. In short, placing of colour in large uniform masses
used in gradation is the groundwork
of all artistic effect in interiors. As I
have said, it is the same rule that gov-
erns pictures, the general tone may be
green or blue, or a division of each,
but to be a perfect and harmonious

view, every detail must relate to one or both of these tints.

In formulating thus far the rules for use of colour in rooms, we have touched upon three principles which are equally binding in interiors, whether of a cottage or a palace; the first is that of colour in relation to light, the second of colour in gradation, and the third of colour in masses.

A house in which walls and ceilings are simply well coloured or covered, has advanced very far toward the home which is the rightful endowment of every human being. The variations of treatment, which pertain to more costly houses, the application of design in borders and frieze spaces, walls, wainscots, and ceilings, are details which will probably call for artistic advice and professional knowledge, since in these things it is easy to err in misapplied decoration. The advance from perfect simplicity to selected and beautiful ornament marks not only the degree of cost but of knowledge which it is in the power of the house-owner to command. The elaboration which is the privilege of more liberal means and the use of artistic experience in decoration on a larger scale.

The smaller house shares in the advantage of beautiful colour, correct principles, and appropriate treatment equally with the more costly. The variations do not falsify principles.

CHAPTER VIII

WALLS, CEILINGS, AND FLOORS

THE true principle of wall treatment is to make the boundary stand for colour and beauty, and not alone for division of space.

As a rule, the colour treatment of a house interior must begin with the walls, and it is fortunate if these are blank and plain as in most new houses with uncoloured ceilings, flat or broken with mouldings to suit the style of the house.

The range of possible treatment is very wide, from simple tones of wall colour against which quiet cottage or domestic city life goes on, to the elaboration of walls of houses of a different grade, where stately pageants are a part of the drama of daily life. But having shown that certain

rules are applicable to both, and indeed necessary to success in both, we
may choose within these rules any
tint or colour which is personally
pleasing.

Rooms with an east or west light
may carry successfully tones of any
shade, without violating fundamental
laws.

The first impression of a room
depends upon the walls. In fact,
rooms are good or bad, agreeable or
ugly in exact accordance with the
wall-quality and treatment. No richness of floor-covering, draperies, or
furniture can minimise their influence.

Perhaps it is for this reason that
the world is full of papers and other
devices for making walls agreeable;
and we cannot wonder at this, when
we reflect that something of the kind
is necessary to the aspect of the room,
and that each room effects for the
individual exactly what the outer

walls of the house effect for the family, they give space for personal privacy and for that reserve of the individual which is the earliest effect of
luxury and comfort.

It is certain that if walls are not
made agreeable there is in them
something of restraint to the eye and
the sense which is altogether disagreeable. Apparent confinement within
given limits, is, on the whole, repug-
nant to either the natural or civilised
man, and for this reason we are constantly tempted to disguise the limit
and to cover the wall in such a way
as shall interest and make us forget
our bounds. In this case, the idea of
decoration is, to make the walls a
barrier of colour only, instead of hard,
unyielding masonry; to take away
the sense of being shut in a box, and
give instead freedom to thought and
pleasure to the sense.

It is the effect of shut-in-ness which

the square and rigid walls of a room
give that makes drapery so effective
and welcome, and which also gives
value to the practice of covering walls
with silks or other textiles. The
softened surface takes away the sense
of restraint. We hang our walls with
pictures, or cover them with textiles,
or with paper which carries design, or
even colour them with pigments—
something—anything, which will disguise a restraining bound, or make it
masquerade as a luxury.

This effort or instinct has set in
motion the machinery of the world.
It has created tapestries and brocades
for castle and palace, and invented
cheap substitutes for these costly products, so that the smallest and poor-
est house as well as the richest can
cover its walls with something pleasant to the eye and suggestive to the
mind.

It is one of the privileges and

LARGE SITTING-ROOM IN "STAR ROCK" COUNTRY HOUSE

opportunities of art to invent these disguises; and to do it so thoroughly and successfully as to content us with facts which would otherwise be disagreeable. And we do, by these various devices, make our walls so hospitable to our thoughts that we take positive and continual pleasure in them.

We do this chiefly, perhaps, by ministering to our instinctive love of colour; which to many temperaments is like food to the hungry, and satisfies as insistent a demand of the mind as food to the body.

At this late period of the world we are the inheritors of many methods of wall disguise, from the primitive weavings or blanket coverings with which nomadic peoples lined the walls of their tents, or the arras which in later days covered the roughness and rudeness of the stone walls of kings and barons, to the pictured

tapestries of later centuries. This latter achievement of art manufacture
has outlived and far outweighed the
others in value, because it more perfectly performs the object of its creation.

Tapestries, for the most part, offer
us a semblance of nature, and cheat
us with a sense of unlimited horizon.
The older tapestries give us, with
this, suggestions of human life and
action in out-of-door scenes sufficiently unrealistic to offer a vague
dream of existence in fields and for-
ests. This effectually diverts our
minds from the confinements of space,
and allows us the freedom of nature.

Probably the true secret of the
never-failing appreciation of tapestries
—from the very beginning of their
history until this day—is this fact of
their suggestiveness; since we find
that damasks of silk or velvet or other
costly weavings, although far surpass-

ing tapestries in texture and concentration of colour, yet lacking their suggestiveness to the mind, can never rival them in the estimation of the world. Unhappily, we cannot count veritable tapestries as a modern recourse in wall-treatment, since we are precluded from the use of genuine ones by their scarcity and cost.

There is undoubtedly a peculiar richness and charm in a tapestry-hung wall which no other wall covering can give; yet they are not entirely appropriate to our time. They belong to the period of windy palaces and enormous enclosures, and are fitted for pageants and ceremonies, and not to our carefully plastered, wind-tight and narrow rooms. Their mission to-day is to reproduce for us in museums and collections the life of yesterday, so full of pomp and almost barbaric lack of domestic comfort. In studios they are certainly appropriate and suggestive, but in private houses except of the princely sort, it is far better to make harmonies with the things of to-day.

Nevertheless if the soul craves tapestries let them be chosen for intrinsic beauty and perfect preservation, instead of accepting the rags of the past and trying to create with them a magnificence which must be incomplete and shabby. Considering, as I do, that tapestries belong to the life and conditions of the past, where the homeless many toiled for the pampered few, and not to the homes of to-day where the man of moderate means expects beauty in his home as confidently as if he were a world ruler, I find it hardly necessary to include them in the list of means of modern decoration, and indeed it is not necessary, since a well-preserved tapestry of a good period, and of a famous manufacturer or origin, is so

costly a purchase that only our boun-
teous and self-indulgent millionaires
would venture to acquire one solely
for purposes of wall decoration.   It
would be purchased as a specimen of
art and not as furnishing.

Yet I know one instance of a library
where a genuine old foliage tapestry
has been cut and fitted to the walls
and between bookcases and doors,
where the wood of the room is in
mahogany, and a great chimney-piece
of Caen stone of Richardson's designing fills nearly one side of the room.
Of course the tapestry is unapproach-
able in effect in this particular place
and with its surroundings.   It has the
richness and softness of velvet, and
the red of the mahogany doors and
furniture finds exactly its foil in the
blue greens and soft browns of the
web, while the polished floor and
velvety antique rugs bring all the
richness of the walls down to one's

feet and to the hearth with its glow of
fire.   But this particular room hardly
makes an example for general following.   It is really a house of state, a
house without children, one in which
public life predominates.

There is a very flagrant far-away
imitation of tapestry which is so far
from being good that it is a wonder
it has had even a moderate success,
imitation which does not even attempt the decorative effect of the
genuine, but substitutes upon an admirably woven cotton or woollen canvas, figure panels, copied from modern French masters, and suggestive of
nothing but bad art.   Yet these panels
are sometimes used (and in fact are
produced for the purpose of being
used) precisely as a genuine tapestry
would be, although the very fact of
pretence in them, brings a feeling
of untruth, quite at variance with the
principles of all good art.   The ob-

jection to pictures transferred to tapestries holds good, even when the
tapestries are genuine.

The great cartoons of Raphael,
still to be seen in the Kensington
Museum, which were drawn and coloured for Flemish weavers to copy,
show a perfect adaptation to the medium of weaving, while the paintings
in the Vatican by the same great
master are entirely inappropriate to
textile reproduction.

A picture cannot be transposed to
different substance and purpose without losing the qualities which make
it valuable. The double effort to be
both a tapestry and a picture is futile,
and brings into disrepute a simple art
of imitation which might become respectable if its capabilities were rightly used.

No one familiar with collections of
tapestries can fail to recognise the
largeness and simplicity of treatment

peculiar to tapestry subjects as contrasted with the elaboration of pictures.

If we grant that in this modern
world of hurry, imitation of tapestries
is legitimate, the important question
is, what are the best subjects, and
what is the best use for such imita-
tions?

The best use is undoubtedly that
of wall-covering; and that was, indeed, the earliest object for which
they were created.   They were woven
to cover great empty spaces of un-
sightly masonry; and they are still in-
finitely useful and beautiful in grand
apartments whose barren spaces are
too large for modern pictures, and
which need the disguise of a suggestion of scenery or pictorial subject.

If tapestries must be painted, let
them by all means follow the style of
the ancient verdure or foliage tapestries, and be used for the same pur-

pose—to cover an otherwise blank wall. This is legitimate, and even beautiful, but it is painting, and should be frankly acknowledged to be such, and no attempt made to have them masquerade as genuine and costly weavings. It is simply and always painting, although in the style and spirit of early tapestries. Productions of this sort, where real skill in textile painting is used, are quite worthy of admiration and respect.

I remember seeing, in the Swedish exhibit of women's work in the Woman's Building at the Columbian Exposition, a screen which had evidently been copied from an old bit of verdure tapestry. At the base were broad-leaved water-plants, each leaf carefully copied in blocks and patches of colour, with even the effect of the little empty space—where one thread passes to the back in weaving, to make room for one of another colour brought forward— imitated by a dot of black to simulate the tiny shadow-filled pen-point of a hole.

Now whether this was art or not I leave to French critics to decide, but it was at least admirable imitation; and any one able to cover the wall spaces between bookcases in a library with such imitation would find them as richly set as if it were veritable tapestry.

This is a very different thing from a painted tapestry, perhaps enlarged from a photograph or engraving of a painting the original of which the tapestry-painter had never even seen —the destiny of which unfortunate copy, changed in size, colour, and all the qualities which gave value to the original, is probably to be hung as a picture in the centre of a space of wall-paper totally antagonistic in colour.

When I see these things I long to
curb the ambition of the unfortunate
tapestry-painter until a course of
study has taught him or her the proper
use of a really useful process; for
whether the object is to produce a
decoration or a simulated tapestry, it
is not attained by these methods.

The ordinary process of painting
in dyes upon a wool or linen fabric
woven in tapestry method, and fix-
ing the colour with heat, enables the
painter—if a true tapestry subject is
chosen and tapestry effects carefully
studied—to produce really effective
and good things, and this opens a
much larger field to the woman decorator than the ordinary unstudied
shams which have thrown what might
become in time a large and useful art-
industry into neglect and disrepute.

I have seen the walls of a library
hung with Siberian linen, stained in
landscape design in the old blues and

greens which give tapestry its decorative value, and found it a delightful
wall-covering.   Indeed we may lay
it down as a principle in decoration
that while we may use and adapt any
decorative *effect* we must not attempt
to make it pass for the thing which
suggested the effect.

Coarse and carefully woven linens,
used as I have indicated, are really far
better than old tapestries for modern houses, because the design can be
adapted to the specific purpose and
the texture itself can be easily cleaned
and is more appropriate to the close
walls and less airy rooms of this century.

For costly wall-decoration, leather
is another of the substances which
have had a past of pomp and magnificence, and carries with it, in addition to beauty, a suggestion of the art
of a race.   Spanish leather, with its
stamping and gilding, is quite as costly

a wall covering as antique or modern tapestry, and far more indestructible. Perhaps it is needlessly durable as a mere vehicle for decoration. At all events Japanese artists and artisans seem to be of this opinion, and have transferred the same kind of decoration to heavy paper, where for some occult reason——although strongly simulating leather——it seems not only not objectionable, but even meritorious. This is because it simply transfers an artistic method from a costly substance, to another which is less so, and the fact may even have some weight that paper is a product of human manufacture, instead of human appropriation of animal life, for surely sentiment has its influence in decoration as in other arts.

Wood panelling is also a form of interior treatment which has come to us by inheritance from the past as well as by right of natural possession.

It has a richness and sober dignity of effect which commends it in large or small interiors, in halls, libraries, and dining-rooms, whether they are public or private; devoted to grand functions, or to the constantly recurring uses of domesticity. Wood is so beautiful a substance in itself, and lends itself to so many processes of ornamentation, that hardly too much can be said of its appropriateness for interior decoration. From the two extremes of plain pine panellings cut into squares or parallelograms by machinery, and covered with paint in tints to match door and window casings, to the most elaborate carvings which back the Cathedral stalls or seats of ecclesiastical dignity, it is always beautiful and generally appropriate in use and effect, and that can hardly be said of any other substance. There are wainscotted rooms in old houses in

PAINTED CANVAS FRIEZE

BUCKRAM FRIEZE FOR DINING-ROOM

Newport, where, under the accumulated paint of one or two centuries,
great panels of old Spanish mahogany
can still be found, not much the
worse for their long eclipse. Such
rooms, in the original brilliancy of
colour and polish, with their parallel
shadings of mahogany-red reflecting
back the firelight from tiled chimney-
places and scattering the play of
dancing flame, must have had a
beauty of colour hard to match in
this day of sober oak and painted
wainscottings.

One of the lessons gained by experience in treatment of house interiors, is that plain, flat tints give
apparent size to small rooms, and
that a satisfying effect in large ones
can be gained by variation of tint or
surface; also, that in a bedroom or
other small room apparent size will
be gained by using a wall covering
which is light rather than dark. Some

difference of tone there must be in large plain surfaces which lie within the level of the eye; or the monotony of a room becomes fatiguing. A plain, painted wall may, it is true, be broken by pictures, or cabinets, or bits of china; anything in short which will throw parts of it into shadow, and illumine other parts with gilded reflections; but even then there will be long, plain spaces above the picture or cabinet line, where blank monotony of tone will be fatal to the general effect of the room.

It is in this upper space, upon a plain painted wall, that a broad line of flat decoration should occur, but on a wall hung with paper or cloth, it is by no means necessary.

Damasked cloths, where the design is shown by the direction of woven threads, are particularly effective and satisfactory as wall-coverings. The

soft surface is luxurious to the imagination, and the play of light and
shadow upon the warp and woof interests the eye, although there is no
actual change of colour.

Too much stress can hardly be laid
upon the variation of tone in wall-
surfaces, since the four walls stand for
the atmosphere of a room.   Tone
means quality of colour.   It may be
light or dark, or of any tint, or variations of tint, but the quality of it
must be soft and charitable, instead
of harsh and uncompromising.

Almost the best of modern inventions for inexpensive wall-coverings
are found in what are called the ingrain papers.   These have a variable
surface, without reflections, and make
not only a soft and impalpable colour
effect, but, on account of their want
of reflection, are good backgrounds
for pictures.

In these papers the colour is produced by a mixture in the mass of paper pulp of atoms of varying tint, which are combined in the substance and make one general tint resulting from the mixture of several. In canvases and textiles, which are a more expensive method of producing almost the same mixed effect, the minute points of brilliance of threads in light and darkness of threads in shadow, combine to produce softness of tone, impossible to pigment because it has but one plain surface, unrelieved by breaking up into light and shadow.

Variation, produced by minute differences, which affect each other and which the eye blends into a general tone, produce quality. It is at the same time soft and brilliant, and is really a popular adaptation of the philosophy of impressionist painters, whose small dabs of pure colour placed in close juxtaposition and fused into one tone by the eye, give the purity and vibration of colour which distinguishes work of that school.

Some skilful painters can stipple one tone upon another so as to produce the same brilliant softness of effect, and when this can be done, oil-colour upon plaster is the best of all treatment for bedrooms since it fulfils all the sanitary and other conditions so necessary in sleeping-rooms. The same effect may be produced if the walls are of rough instead of smooth plaster, so that the small inequalities of surface give light and shadow as in textiles; upon such surfaces a pleasant tint in flat colour is always good. Painted burlaps and certain Japanese papers prepared with what may be called a textile or canvas surface give the same effect, and indeed quality of tint and tone is far more easily obtained in wall-coverings or applied materials than in paint, because in most wall-coverings there are variations of tint produced in the very substance of the material.

This matter of variation without contrast in wall-surface, is one of the most important in house decoration, and has led to the increased use of textiles in houses where artistic effects have been carefully studied and are considered of importance.

Of course wall-paper must continue to be the chief means of wall-covering, on account of its cheapness, and because it is the readiest means of sheathing a plaster surface; and a continuous demand for papers of good and nearly uniform colour, and the sort of inconspicuous design which fits them for modest interiors will have the effect of increasing the manufacture of desirable and artistic things.

In the meantime one should carefully avoid the violently coloured papers which are made only to sell; materials which catch the eye of the inexperienced and tempt them into the buying of things which are productive of lasting unrest. It is in the nature of positive masses and strongly contrasting colours to produce this effect.

If one is unfortunate enough to occupy a room of which the walls are covered with one of these glaring designs, and circumstances prevent a radical change, the simplest expedient is to cover the whole surface with a kalsomine or chalk-wash, of some agreeable tint. This will dry in an hour or two and present a nearly uniform surface, in which the printed design of the paper, if it appears at all, will be a mere suggestion. Papers where the design is carried in colour only a few shades darker than the background, are also safe, and—if the design is a good one—often very desirable for halls and dining-rooms. In skilfully printed papers of the sort the design often has the effect of a mere shadow-play of form.

Of course in the infinite varieties of use and the numberless variations of personal taste, there are, and should be, innumerable differences in application of both colour and materials to interiors. There are differences in the use of rooms which may make a sense of perfect seclusion desirable, as, for instance, in libraries, or rooms used exclusively for evening gatherings of the family. In such semi-private rooms the treatment should give a sense of close family life rather than space, while in drawing-rooms it should be exactly the reverse, and this effect is easily secured by competent use of colour.

CHAPTER IX

LOCATION OF THE HOUSE

BESIDES the difference in treatment demanded by different use of rooms—the character of the decoration of the whole house will be influenced by its situation. A house in the country or a house in town; a house by the sea-shore or a house situated in woods and fields require stronger or less strong colour, and even different tints, according to situation. The decoration itself may be much less conventional in one place than in another, and in country houses much and lasting charm is derived from design and colour in perfect harmony with nature's surroundings. Whatever decorative design is used in wall-coverings or in curtains or hangings will be far more effective if it bears some relation to the surroundings and position of the house.

If the house is by the sea the walls should repeat with many variations the tones of sea and sand and sky; the gray-greens of sand-grasses; the blues which change from blue to green with every cloud-shadow; the pearl tints which become rose in the morning or evening light, and the browns and olives of sea mosses and lichens. This treatment of colour will make the interior of the house a part of the great out-of-doors and create a harmony between the artificial shelter and nature.

There is philosophy in following, as far as the limitations of simple colour will allow, the changeableness and fluidity of natural effects along the shore, and allowing the mood of the brief summer life to fall into entire harmony with the dominant

expression of the sea. Blues and
greens and pinks and browns should
all be kept on a level with out-of-
door colour, that is, they should not
be too deep and strong for harmony
with the sea and sky, and if, when
harmonious colour is once secured,
most of the materials used in the
furnishing of the house are chosen
because their design is based upon, or
suggested by, sea-forms, an impression
is produced of having entered into
complete and perfect harmony with
the elements and aspects of nature.
The artificialities of life fall more and
more into the background, and one
is refreshed with a sense of having
established entirely harmonious and
satisfactory relations with the surroundings of nature.   I remember a
doorway of a cottage by the sea,
where the moulding which made a
part of the frame was an orderly line
of carved cockle-shells, used as a bor-

der, and this little touch of recog-
nition of its sea-neighbours was not
only decorative in itself, but gave
even the chance visitor a sort of in-
terpretation of the spirit of the interior life.

Suppose, on the other hand, that
the summer house is placed in the
neighbourhood of fields and trees and
mountains; it will be found that
strong and positive treatment of the
interior is more in harmony with the
outside landscape.   Even heavier furniture looks fitting where the house is
surrounded with massive tree-growths;
and deeper and purer colours can be
used in hangings and draperies.   This
is due to the more positive colouring
of a landscape than of a sea-view.
The masses of strong and slightly
varying green in foliage, the red,
brown, or vivid greens of fields and
crops, the dark lines of tree-trunks
and branches, as well as the unchang-

ing forms of rock and hillside, call for a corresponding strength of interior effect.

It is a curious fact, also, that where a house is surrounded by myriads of small natural forms of leaves and flowers and grasses, plain spaces of colour in interiors, or spaces where form is greatly subordinated to colour, are more grateful to the eye than prominently decorated surface. A repetition of small natural forms like the shells and sea-mosses, which are for the most part hidden under lengths of liquid blue, is pleasing and suggestive by the sea; but in the country, where form is prominent and positive and prints itself constantly upon both mental and bodily vision, unbroken colour surfaces are found to be far more agreeable.

It will be seen that the principles of appropriate furnishing and adornment in house interiors depend upon circumstances and natural surroundings as well as upon the character and pursuits of the family who are to be lodged, and that the final charm of the home is attained by a perfect adaptation of principles to existing conditions both of nature and humanity.

In cottages of the character we are considering, furniture should be simpler and lighter than in houses intended for constant family living. Chairs and sofas should be without elaborate upholstery and hangings, and cushions can be appropriately made of some well-coloured cotton or linen material which wind, and sun, and dampness cannot spoil, and of which the freshness can always be restored by laundering. These are general rules, appropriate to all summer cottages, and to these it may be added, that a house which is to be closed for six or eight months in the year should really, to be consistent, be inexpensively furnished. These general rules are intended only to emphasise the fact that in houses which are to become in the truest sense homes—that is, places of habitation which represent the inhabitants, directions or rules for beautiful colour and arrangement of interiors, must always follow the guiding incidents of class and locality.

AS ceilings are in reality a part of the wall, they must always be considered in connection with room interiors, but their influence upon the beauty of the average house is so small, that their treatment is a comparatively easy problem.

In simple houses with plaster ceilings the tints to be used are easily decided. The rule of gradation of colour from floor to ceiling prescribes for the latter the lightest tone of the gradation, and as the ceiling stands for light, and should actually reflect light into the room, the philosophy of this arrangement of colours is obvious. It is not, however, an invariable rule that the ceiling should carry the same tint as the wall, even in a much lighter tone, although greater harmony and restfulness of effect is produced in this way. A ceiling of cream white will harmonise well with almost any tint upon the walls, and at the same time give an effect of air and light in the room. It is also a good ground for ornament in elaborately decorated ones.

If the walls are covered with a light wall-paper which carries a floral design, it is a safe rule to make the ceiling of the same colour but a lighter shade of the background of the paper, but it is not by any means good art to carry a flower design over the ceiling. One sometimes sees instances of this in the bedrooms of fairly good houses, and the effect is naturally that of bringing the ceiling apparently almost to one's head, or at all events, of producing a very unrestful effect.

A wood ceiling in natural colour

is always a good feature in a room of
defined or serious purpose, like a hall,
dining-room, or library, because in
such rooms the colour of the side
walls is apt to be strong enough to
balance it.   Indeed a wooden ceiling
has always the merit of being secure
in its place, and even where the walls
are light can be painted so as to be
in harmony with them.   Plaster as a
ceiling for bedrooms is open to the
objection of a possibility of its de-
taching itself from the lath, especially
in old houses, and in these it is well
to have them strengthened with flat
mouldings of wood put on in regular
squares, or even in some geometrical
design, and painted with the ceiling.
This gives security as well as a certain elaborateness of effect not without its value.

For the ordinary, or comparatively
inexpensive home, we need not consider the ceiling an object for serious

study, because it is so constantly out
of the line of sight, and because its
natural colourless condition is no bar
to the general colour-effect.

In large rooms this condition is
changed, for in a long perspective
the ceiling comes into sight and consciousness. There would be a sense
of barrenness and poverty in a long
stretch of plain surface or unbroken
colour over a vista of decorated wall,
and accordingly the ceilings of large
and important rooms are generally
broken by plaster mouldings or architectural ornament.

In rooms of this kind, whether in
public or private buildings, decorative
painting has its proper and appropriate place. A painted ceiling, no
matter how beautiful, is quite superfluous and indeed absolutely lost in a
room where size prevents its being
brought into the field of the eye by
the lowering of long perspective lines,

but when the size of the room gives
unusual length of ceiling, no effect of
decoration is so valuable and precious.   Colour and gilding upon a
ceiling, when well sustained by fine
composition or treatment, is undoubtedly the highest and best achievement
of the decorative painter's art.

Such a ceiling in a large and stately
drawing-room, where the walls are
hung with silk which gives broken
indications of graceful design in play
of light upon the texture, is one of
the most successful of both modern
as well as antique methods of decoration.   It has come down in direct
succession of practice to the school of
French decoration of to-day, and has
been adopted into American fashion
in its full and complete practice without sufficient adaptation to American
circumstances.   If it were modified
by these, it is capable of absorbing
other and better qualities than those

of mere fashion and brilliance, as we see in occasional instances in some beautiful American houses, where the ceilings have been painted, and the textiles woven with an almost imaginative appropriateness of subject. Such ceilings as this belong, of course, to the efforts of the mural or decorative painter, who, in conjunction with the decorator, or architect, has studied the subject as connected with its surroundings.

CHAPTER XI

FLOORS AND FLOOR-COVERINGS

ALTHOUGH in ordinary sequence the colouring of floors comes after that of walls, the fact that—in important houses—costly and elaborate floors of mosaic or of inlaid wood form part of the architect's plan, makes it necessary to consider the effect of inherent or natural colours of such floors, in connection with applied colour-schemes in rooms.

Mosaic floors, being as a rule confined to halls in private houses, need hardly be considered in this relation, and costly wood floors are almost necessarily confined to the yellows of the natural woods. These yellows range from pale buff to olive, and are not as a rule inharmonious with any other tint, although they often lack sufficient strength or intensity to hold their own with stronger tints of walls and furniture.

As it is one of the principles of colour in a house that the floor is the foundation of the room, this weakness of colour in hard-wood floors must be acknowledged as a disadvantage. The floors should certainly be able to support the room in colour as well as in construction. It must be the strongest tint in the room, and yet it must have the unobtrusiveness of strength. This makes floor treatment a more difficult problem, or one requiring more thought than is generally supposed, and explains why light rooms are more successful with hard-wood floors than medium or very dark ones.

There are many reasons, sanitary as well as economic, why hard-wood floors should not be covered in ordinary dwelling-houses; and when the pores of the wood are properly filled, and the surface kept well polished, it is not only good as a fact, but as an effect, as it reflects surrounding tints, and does much to make up for lack of sympathetic or related colour. Yet it will be found that in almost every case of successful colour-treatment in a room, something must be added in the way of floor-covering to give it the sense of completeness and satisfaction which is the result of a successful scheme of decoration.

The simplest way of doing this is to cover enough of the space with rugs to attract the eye, and restore the balance lost by want of strength of colour in the wood. Sometimes one or two small rugs will do this, and these may be of almost any tint which includes the general one of the room, even if the general tint is not prominent in the rug. If the use or

SQUARE HALL IN CITY HOUSE

luxury of the room requires more covered space, it is better to use one rug of a larger size than several small and perhaps conflicting ones. Of course in this the general tone of the rug must be chosen for its affinity to the tone of the room, but that affinity secured, any variations of colour occurring in the design are apt to add to the general effect.

A certain amount of contrast to prevailing colour is an advantage, and the general value of rugs in a scheme of decoration is that they furnish this contrast in small masses or divisions, so well worked in with other tints and tones that it makes its effect without opposition to the general plan.

Thus, in a room where the walls are of a pale shade of copper, the rugs should bring in a variety of reds which would be natural parts of the same scale, like lower notes in the octave; and yet should add patches of relative blues and harmonising greens; possibly also, deep gold, and black and white;—the latter in minute forms and lines which only accent or enrich the general effect.

It is really an interesting problem, why the strong colours generally used in Oriental rugs should harmonise so much better with weaker tints in walls and furniture than even the most judiciously selected carpets can possibly do. It is true there are bad Oriental rugs, very bad ones, just as there may be a villain in any congregation of the righteous, but certainly the long centuries of Eastern manufacture, reaching back to the infancy of the world, have given Eastern nations secrets not to be easily mastered by the people of later days.

But if we cannot tell with certainty why good rugs fit all places and circumstances, while any other thing of mortal manufacture must have its place carefully prepared for it, we may perhaps assume to know why the most beautiful of modern carpets are not as easily managed and as successful.

In the first place having explained that some contrast, some fillip of opposing colour, something which the artist calls *snap*, is absolutely required in every successful colour scheme, we shall see that if we are to get this by simple means of a carpet, we must choose one which carries more than one colour in its composition, and colour introduced as design must come under the laws of mechanical manufacture; that is, it must come in as *repeating* design, and here comes in the real difficulty. The same forms and the same colours must come in in the same way in every yard, or every half or three-

quarter yard of the carpet. It follows, then, that it must be evenly
sprinkled or it must regularly mean-
der over every yard or half yard of
the surface; and this regularity re-
solves itself into spots, and spots are
unendurable in a scheme of colour.
So broad a space as the floor of a
room cannot be covered by sections
of constantly repeated design without
producing a spotty effect, although it
can be somewhat modified by the
efforts of the good designer. Nevertheless, in spite of his best knowledge
and intention, the difficulty remains.
There is no one patch of colour
larger than another, or more irregular in form. There is nothing which
has not its exact counterpart at an
exact distance—north, south, east
and west, or northeast, southeast,
northwest and southwest—and this
is why a carpet with good design and
excellent colour becomes unbearable

in a room of large size. In a small
room where there are not so many
repeats, the effect is not as bad, but
in a large room the monotonous
repetition is almost without remedy.

Of course there are certain laws of
optics and ingenuities of composition
which may palliate this effect, but
the fact remains that the floor should
be covered in a way which will leave
the mind tranquil and the eye satisfied, and this is hard to accomplish
with what is commonly known as a
figured carpet.

If carpet is to be used, it seems,
then, that the simplest way is to
select a good monochrome in the
prevailing tint of the room, but several shades darker. Not an absolutely plain surface, but one broken
with some unobtrusive design or pattern in still darker darks and lighter
lights than the general tone. In this
case we shall have the room har-

monious, it is true, but lacking the element which provokes admiration —the enlivening effect of contrast. This may be secured by making the centre or main part of the carpet comparatively small, and using a very wide and important border of contrasting colour—a border so wide as to make itself an important part of the carpet. In large rooms this plan does not entirely obviate the difficulty, as it leaves the central space still too large and impressive to remain unbroken; but the remedy may be found in the use of hearthrugs or skin-rugs, so placed as to seem necessities of use.

As I have said before, contrast on a broad scale can be secured by choosing carpets of an entirely different tone from the wall, and this is sometimes expedient. For instance, as contrast to a copper-coloured wall, a softly toned green carpet is nearly always successful. This one colour, green, is always safe and satisfactory in a floor-covering, provided the walls are not too strong in tone, and provided that the green in the carpet is not too green. Certain brownish greens possess the quality of being in harmony with every other colour. They are the most peaceable shades in the colour-world—the only ones without positive antipathies. Green in all the paler tones can claim the title of peace-maker among colours, since all the other tints will fight with something else, but never with green of a corresponding or even of a much greater strength. Of course this valuable quality, combined with a natural restfulness of effect, makes it the safest of ordinary floor-coverings.

In bedrooms with polished floors and light walls good colour-effects can be secured without carpets, but if the floors are of pine and need covering, no better general effect can be secured than that of plain or mixed ingrain filling, using with it Oriental hearth and bedside rugs.

The entire second floor of a house can in that case be covered with carpet in the accommodating tint of green mentioned, leaving the various colour-connections to be made with differently tinted rugs. Good pine floors well fitted and finished can be stained to harmonise with almost any tint used in furniture or upon the wall.

I remember a sea-side chamber in a house where the mistress had great natural decorative ability, and so much cultivation as to prevent its running away with her, where the floor was stained a transparent olive, like depths of sea-water, and here and there a floating sea-weed, or a form of sea-life faintly outlined within the colour. In this room, which seemed wide open to the sea and air, even when the windows were closed, the walls were of a faint greenish blue, like what is called *dead* turquoise, and the relation between floor and walls was so perfect that it remained with me to this day as a crowning instance of satisfaction in colour.

It is perhaps more difficult to convey an idea of happy choice or selection of floor-colour than of walls, because it is relative to walls. It must relate to what has already been done. But in recapitulation it is safe to say, first, that in choosing colour for a room, soft and medium tints are better than positively dark or bright ones, and that walls should be unobtrusive in design as well as colour; secondly, that floors, if of the same tint as walls, should be much darker; and that they should be *made apparent* by means of this strength of colour, or by the addition of rugs or borders, although the relation between walls and floor must be carefully preserved and perfectly unmistakable, for it is the perfection of this relation of one colour to another which makes home decoration an art.

There is still a word to be said as to floor-coverings, which relates to healthful housekeeping instead of art, and that is, that in all cases where carpets or mattings are used, they should be in rug form, not fitted in to irregular floor-spaces; so as to be frequently and easily lifted and cleaned. The great, and indeed the only, objection to the use of mattings in country or summer houses, is the difficulty of frequent lifting, and removal of accumulated dust, which has sifted through to the floor—but if fine hemp-warp mattings are used, and sewn into squares which cover the floor sufficiently, it is an ideal summer floor-covering, as it can be rolled and removed even more easily than a carpet, and there is a dust-shedding quality in it which commends itself to the housekeeper.

CHAPTER XII

DRAPERIES

DRAPERIES are not always considered as a part of furnishings,
yet in truth——as far as decorative necessities are concerned——they should
come immediately after wall and floor
coverings. The householder who is
in haste to complete the arrangement of the home naturally thinks first
of chairs, sofas, and tables, because
they come into immediate personal
use, but if draperies are recognised
as a necessary part of the beauty of
the house it is worth while to study
their appropriate character from the
first. They have in truth much more
to do with the effect of the room
than chairs or sofas, since these are
speedily sat upon and pass out of

notice, while draperies or portières
are in the nature of pictures—hanging in everybody's sight. As far as
the element of beauty is concerned, a
room having good colour, attractive
and interesting pictures, and beautiful
draperies, is already furnished. Whatever else goes to the making of it
may be also beautiful, but it must be
convenient and useful, while in the
selection of draperies, beauty, both
relative and positive, is quite untram-
melled.

As in all other furnishings, from
the æsthetic point of view colour is
the first thing to be considered. As
a rule it should follow that of the
walls, a continuous effect of colour
with variation of form and surface being a valuable and beautiful thing to
secure. To give the full value of
variation—where the walls are plain
one should choose a figured stuff for
curtains; where the wall is papered,

or covered with figures, a plain material should be used.

There is one exception to this rule and this is in the case of walls hung with damask. Here it is best to use the same material for curtains, as the effect is obtained by the difference between the damask hung in folds, with the design indistinguishable, or stretched flat upon a wall-surface, where it is plainly to be seen and felt. Even where damask is used upon the walls, if exactly the same shade of colour can be found in satin or velvet, the plain material in drapery will enhance the value of design on the walls.

This choice or selection of colour applies to curtains and portières as simple adjuncts of furnishing, and not to such pieces of drapery as are in themselves works of art. When a textile becomes a work of art it is in a measure a law unto itself, and has

as much right to select its own colour as if it were a picture instead of
a portière, in fact if it is sufficiently
important, the room must follow instead of leading. This may happen
in the case of some priceless old
embroidery, some relic of that peace-
ful past, when hours and days flowed
contentedly into a scheme of art and
beauty, without a thought of com-
petitive manufacture. It might be
difficult to subdue the spirit of a
modern drawing-room into harmony
with such a work of art, but if it
were done, it would be a very shrine
of restfulness to the spirit.

Fortunately many ancient marvels
of needlework were done upon white
satin, and this makes them easily
adaptable to any light scheme of colour, where they may appear indeed
as guests of honour—invited from
the past to be courted by the present. It is not often that such pieces

are offered as parts of a scheme of modern decoration, and the fingers of to-day are too busy or too idle for their creation, yet it sometimes happens that a valuable piece of drapery of exceptional colour belongs by inheritance or purchase to the fortunate householder, and in this case it should be used as a picture would be, for an independent bit of decoration.

To return to simple things, the rule of contrast as applied to papered walls, covered with design, ordains that the curtains should undoubtedly be plain and of the most pronounced tint used in the paper. If the walls of a room are simply tinted or painted, figured stuffs of the same general tone, or printed silks, velvets, or cottons in which the predominant tint corresponds with that of the wall should be used. These relieve the simplicity of the walls, and give the desirable variation.

Transparent silk curtains are of great value in colouring the light which enters the room, and these should be used in direct reference to the light. If the room is dark or cold in its exposure, to hang the windows with sun-coloured silk or muslin will cheat the eye and imagination into the idea that it is a sunny room. If, on the contrary, there is actual sunshine in the room, a pervading tint of rose-colour or delicate green may be given by inner curtains of either of those colours. These are effects, however, for which rules can hardly be given, since the possible variations must be carefully studied, unless, indeed, they are the colour-strokes of some one who has that genius for combination or contrast of tints which we call " colour sense."

After colour in draperies come texture and quality, and these need hardly be discussed in the case of silken fabrics, because silk fibre has inherent qualities of tenacity of tint and flexibility of substance. Pure silk, that is silk unstiffened with gums, no matter how thickly and heavily it is woven, is soft and yielding and will fall into folds without sharp angles. This quality of softness is in its very substance. Even a single unwoven thread of silk will drop gracefully into loops, where a cotton or linen or even a woollen thread will show stiffness.

Woollen fibre seems to acquire softness as it is gathered into yarns and woven, and will hang in folds with almost the same grace as silk; but unfortunately they are favourite pasture grounds as well as burying-places for moths, and although these co-inhabitants of our houses come to a speedy resurrection, they devour their very graves, and leave our woollen

draperies irremediably damaged. It
is a pity that woollen fabrics should
in this way be made undesirable for
household use, for they possess in a
great degree the two most valuable
qualities of silk : colour-tenacity and
flexibility. If one adopts woollen curtains and portières, constant " vigilance is the price of safety," and considering that vigilance is required
everywhere and at all times in the
household, it is best to reduce the
quantity whenever it is possible.

This throws us back upon cottons
and linens for inexpensive hangings,
and in all the thousand forms in
which these two fibres are manufactured it would seem easy to choose
those which are beautiful, durable,
and appropriate. But here we are
met at the very threshold of choice
with the two undesirable qualities of
fugitive colour, and stiffness of texture. Something in the nature of

cotton makes it inhospitable to dyes.
If it receives them it is with a protest, and an evident intention of
casting them out at the earliest op-
portunity—it makes, it is true, one
or two exceptions. It welcomes indigo dye and will never quite relin-
quish its companionship; once re-
ceived, it will carry its colours
through all its serviceable life, and
when it is finally ready to fall into
dust, it is still loyally coloured by its
influence. If it is cheated, as we
ourselves are apt to be, into accepting spurious indigo, made up of
chemical preparations, it speedily dis-
covers the cheat and refuses its colouring. Perhaps this sympathy is
due to a vegetable kinship and likeness of experience, for where cotton
will grow, indigo will also flourish.

In printed cottons or chintzes,
there is a reasonable amount of
fidelity to colour, and if chintz cur-

tains are well chosen, and lined to protect them from the sun, their attractiveness bears a fair proportion to their durability.

An interlining of some strong and tried colour will give a very soft and subtle daylight effect in a room, but this is, of course, lost in the evening. The expedient of an under colour in curtain linings will sometimes give delightful results in plain or un-printed goods, and sometimes a lining with a strong and bold design will produce a charming shadow effect upon a tinted surface——of course each new experiment must be tried before one can be certain of its effect, and, in fact, there is rather an ex-citing uncertainty as to results. Yet there are infinite possibilities to the householder who has what is called the artistic instinct and the leisure and willingness to experiment, and experiments need not be limited to prints or to cottons, for wonderful combinations of colour are possible in silks where light is called in as an influence in the composition. One must, however, expect to forego these effects except in daylight, but as artificial light has its own subtleties of effect, the one can be balanced against the other. In my own country-house I have used the two strongest colours—red and blue—in this doubled way, with delightful effect. The blue, which is the face colour, presenting long, pure folds of blue, with warmed reddish shadows between, while at sunset, when the rays of light are level, the variations are like a sunset sky.

It will be seen by these suggestions that careful selection, and some knowledge of the qualities of different dyes, will go far toward modifying the want of permanence of colour and lack of reflection in cottons; the other quality of stiffness, or want of flexibility, is occasionally overcome by methods of weaving. Indeed, if the manufacturer or weaver had a clear idea of excellence in this respect, undoubtedly the natural inflexibility of fibre could be greatly overcome.

There is a place waiting in the world of art and decoration for what in my own mind I call "the missing textile." This is by no means a fabric of cost, for among its other virtues it must possess that of cheapness. To meet an almost universal want it should combine inexpensiveness, durability, softness, and absolute fidelity of colour, and these four qualities are not to be found in any existing textile. Three of them — cheapness, strength, and colour — were possessed by the old-fashioned true indigo-blue denim — the delightful blue which faded into something as near the col-

our of the flower of grass, as dead
vegetable material can approach that
which is full of living juices—the
possession of these three qualities
doubled and trebled the amount of its
manufacture until it lost one of them
by masquerading in aniline indigo.

Many of our ordinary cotton
manufactures are strong and inexpensive, and a few of them have the
flexibility which denim lacks.   It was
possessed in an almost perfect degree
by the Canton, or fleeced, flannels,
manufactured so largely a few years
ago,   and   called   art-drapery.   It
lacked colour, however, for the various dyes given to it during its brief
period of favouritism were not colour; they were merely *tint*.   That
strong, good word, colour, could not
be applied to the mixed and evanescent dyes with which this soft
and estimable material clothed itself
withal.   It was, so to speak, inverte-

brate—it had no backbone. Besides this lack of colour stanchness, it had another fault which helped to overbalance its many virtues. It was fatally attractive to fire. Its soft, fluffy surface seemed to reach out toward flame, and the contact once made, there ensued one flash of instantaneous blaze, and the whole surface, no matter if it were a table-cover, a hanging, or the wall covering a room, was totally destroyed. Yet as one must have had or heard of such a disastrous experience to fear and avoid it, this proclivity alone would not have ended its popularity. It was probably the evanescent character of what was called its "art-colour" which ended the career of an estimable material, and if the manufacturers had known how to eliminate its faults and adapt its virtues, it might still have been a flourishing textile.

In truth, we do not often stop to
analyse the reasons of prolonged
popular favour; yet nothing is more
certain than that there is reason, and
good reason, for fidelity in public
taste.   Popular liking, if continued,
is always founded upon certain in-
controvertible virtues.   If a manufacture cannot hold its own for ever
in public favour, it is because it fails
in some important particular to be
what it should be.   Products of the
loom must have lasting virtues if they
would secure lasting esteem.   Blue
denim had its hold upon public use
principally for the reason that it possessed a colour superior to all the
chances and accidents of its varied
life.   It is true it was a colour which
commended itself to general liking,
yet if as stanch and steadfast a green
or red could be imparted to an equally
cheap and durable fabric, it would
find as lasting a place in public favour.

It is quite possible that in the near future domestic weavings may come to the aid of the critical house-furnisher, so that the qualities of strength and pliability may be united with colour which is both water-fast and sun-fast, and that we shall be able to order not only the kind of material, but the exact shade of colour necessary to the perfection of our houses.

To be washable as well as durable is also a great point in favour of cotton textiles. The English chintzes with which the high post bedsteads of our foremothers were hung had a yearly baptism of family soap-suds, and came from it with their designs of gaily-crested, almost life-size pheasants, sitting upon inadequate branches, very little subdued by the process. Those were not days of colour-study; and harmony, applied to things of sight instead of conduct, was not looked for; but when we copy the beautiful old furniture of that day, we may as well demand with it the quality of washableness and cleanableness which went with all its belongings.

It is always a wonder to the masculine, that the feminine mind has such an ineradicable love of draperies. The man despises them, but to the woman they are the perfecting touch of the home, hiding or disguising all the sharp angles of windows and doors, and making of them opportunities of beauty. It is the same instinct with which she tries to cover the hard angles and facts of daily life and make of them virtuous incitements. As long as the woman rules, house-curtains will be a joy and delight to her. Something in their soft protection, grace of line, and possible beauty of colour appeals to her as no other household belonging has the power to do.

The long folds of the straight
hanging curtain are far more beautiful
than the looped and festooned crea-
tions which were held in vogue by
some previous generations, and indeed
are still dear to the hearts of professional upholsterers. The simpler the
treatment, the better the effect, since
natural rather than distorted line is
more restful and enjoyable. Quality, colour, and simple graceful lines
are quite sufficient elements of value
in these important adjuncts of house
furnishing and decoration.

CHAPTER XIII

FURNITURE

ALTHOUGH the forms and varieties of furniture are infinite, they can easily be classified first into the two great divisions of good and bad, and after that into kinds and styles; but no matter how good the different specimens may be, or to what style they may belong, each one is subject again to the ruling of fitness. Detached things may be both thoroughly pleasing and thoroughly good in themselves, but unless they are appropriate to the place where, and purpose for which they are used, they will not be beautiful.

It is well to reiterate that the use to which a room is put must always govern its furnishing and in a measure its colour, and that whatever we

COLONIAL CHAIRS AND SOFA (BELONGING TO MRS. RUTH MCENERY STUART)

put in it must be placed there because it is appropriate to that use, and because it is needed for completeness. It is misapplication which makes much of what is called " artistic furnishing" ridiculous. An old-fashioned brass preserving-kettle and a linen or wool spinning-wheel are in place and appropriate pieces of furnishing for a studio; the one for colour, and the other for form, and because also they may serve as models; but they are sadly out of place in a modern city house, or even in the parlour of a country cottage.

We all recognise the fact that a room carefully furnished in one style makes a oneness of impression; whereas if things are brought together heterogeneously, even if each separate thing is selected for its own special virtue and beauty, the feeling of enjoyment will be far less complete.

There is a certain kinship in pieces of furniture made or originated at the same period and fashioned by a prevailing sentiment of beauty, which makes them harmonious when brought together; and if our minds are in sympathy with that period and style of expression, it becomes a great pleasure to use it as a means of expression for ourselves. Whatever appeals to us as the best or most beautiful thought in manufacture we have a right to adopt, but we should study to understand the circumstances of its production, in order to do justice to it and ourselves, since style is evolved from surrounding influences. It would seem also that its periods and origin should not be too far removed from the interests and ways of our own time, and incongruous with it, because it would be impossible to carry an utterly foreign period or method of thought into all the intimacies of domestic life. The fad of furnishing different rooms in different periods of art, and in the fashion of nations and peoples whose lives are totally dissimilar, may easily be carried too far, and the spirit of home, and even of beauty, be lost. Of course this applies to small, and not to grand houses, which are always exceptions to the purely domestic idea.

There are many reasons why one should be in sympathy with what is called the "colonial craze"; not only because colonial days are a part of our history, but because colonial furniture and decorations were derived directly from the best period of English art. Its original designers were masters who made standards in architectural and pictorial as well as household art. The Adams brothers, to whom many of the best forms of the period are referable,

were great architects as well as great
designers. Even so distinguished a
painter as Hogarth delighted in com-
posing symmetrical forms for furniture,
and preached persistently the beauty
of curved instead of rectangular lines.
It was, in fact, a period in which
superior minds expressed themselves
in material forms, when Flaxman,
Wedgwood, Chippendale and many
others of their day, true artists in
form, wrote their thoughts in wood,
stone, and pottery, and bequeathed
them to future ages. Certainly the
work of such minds in such company
must outlast mere mechanical efforts.
It is interesting to note, that many of
the Chippendale chairs keep in their
under construction the square and
simple forms of a much earlier period,
while the upper part, the back, and
seats are carved into curves and flori-
ated designs. One cannot help won-
dering whether this square solidity

was simply a reminiscence or persistence of earlier forms, or a conscious return to the most direct principles of weight-bearing constructions.

All furniture made under primitive conditions naturally depends upon perpendicular and horizontal forms, because uninfluenced construction considers first of all the principle of strength; but under the varied influences of the Georgian period one hardly expects fidelity to first principles. New England carpenters and cabinet-makers who had wrought under the masters of carpentry and cabinet-work in England brought with them not only skill to fashion, but the very patterns and drawings from which Chippendale and Sheraton furniture had been made in England. Our English forefathers were very fond of the St. Domingo mahogany, brought back in the ship-bottoms of English traders, but the

English workmen who made furniture in the new world, while they adopted this foreign wood, were not slow to appreciate the wild cherry, and the different maples and oak and nut woods which they found in America. They were woods easy to work, and apt to take on polish and shining surface. The cabinet-makers liked also the abnormal specimens of maple where the fibre grew in close waves, called *curled* maple, as well as the great roots flecked and spotted with minute knots, known as dotted maple.

All these things went into colonial furniture, so beautifully cut, so carefully dowelled and put together, so well made, that many of the things have become heirlooms in the families for which they were constructed. I remember admiring a fine old cherry book-case in Mr. Lowell's library at Cambridge, and being told by the poet that it had belonged to his grandfather. When I spoke of the comparative rarity of such possessions he answered: " Oh, anyone can have his grandfather's furniture if he will wait a hundred years!"

Nevertheless, with modern methods of manufacture it is by no means certain that a hundred years will secure possession of the furniture we buy to-day to our grandchildren. In those early days it was not uncommon, it was indeed the custom, for some one of the men who were called " journeymen cabinet-makers "—that is, men who had served their time and learned their trade, but had not yet settled down to a fixed place and shop of their own—to take up an abode in the house with the family which had built it, for a year, or even two or three years, carrying on the work in some out-house or dependence, choosing and seasoning the

wood, and measuring the furniture
for the spaces where it was to stand.

There was a fine fitness in such furnishing; it was as if the different
pieces actually grew where they were
placed, and it is small wonder that
so built and fashioned they should
possess almost a human interest.
Direct and special thought and effort
were incorporated with the furniture
from the very first, and it easily explains the excellences and finenesses
of its fashioning.

There is an interesting house in
Flushing, Long Island, where such
furniture still stands in the rooms
where it was put together in 1664,
and where it is so fitted to spaces it
has filled during the passing centuries,
that it would be impossible to carry it
through the narrow doors and passages,
which, unlike our present halls, were
made for the passing to and fro of
human beings, and not of furniture.

COLONIAL MANTEL AND ENGLISH HOB-GRATE (SITTING-ROOM IN MRS. CANDACE
WHEELER'S HOUSE)

It is this kind of interest which attaches us to colonial furniture and adds to the value of its beauty and careful adaptation to human convenience. In the roomy "high boys" which we find in old houses there are places for everything. They were made for the orderly packing and keeping of valuable things, in closetless rooms, and they were made without projecting corners and cornices, because life was lived in smaller spaces than at present. They were the best product of a thoughtful time—where if manufacture lacked some of the machinery and appliances of to-day, it was at least not rushed by breathless competition, but could progress slowly in careful leisure. Of course we cannot all have colonial furniture, and indeed it would not be according to the spirit of our time, for the arts of our own day are to be encouraged and fostered—but we can buy the best of the things which are made in our time, the best in style, in intention, in fittingness, and above all in carefulness and honesty of construction.

For some reason the quality of durability seems to be wanting in modern furniture. Our things are fashioned of the same woods, but something in the curing or preparation of them has weakened the fibre and made it brittle. Probably the gradual evaporation of the tree-juices which old-time cabinet-makers were willing to wait for, left the shrunken sinews of the wood in better condition than is possible with our hurried and violent kiln-dried methods. What is gained in time in the one place is lost in another. Nature refuses to enter into our race for speedy completion, and if we hurry her natural processes we shorten our lease of ownership.

As a very apt illustration of this

fact, I remember coming into possession some twenty years ago of an oak
chair which had stood, perhaps, for
more than two hundred years in a
Long Island farm-house. When I
found it, it had been long relegated
to kitchen use and was covered with
a crust of variously coloured paints
which had accumulated during the
two centuries of its existence. The
fashion of it was rare, and had probably been evolved by some early
American cabinet-maker, for while it
had all and even more than the grace
of the high-backed Chippendale patterns, it was better fitted to the
rounded surfaces of the human body.
It was a spindle chair with a slightly
hollowed seat, the rim of the back
rounded to a loop which was continued into arm-rests, which spread
into thickened blades for hand-rests.
Being very much in love with the
grace and ease of it, I took it to a

manufacturer to be reproduced in mahogany, who, with a far-sighted sagacity, flooded the market with that particular pattern.

We are used—and with good reason—to consider mahogany as a durable wood, but of the half-dozen of mahogany copies of the old oak chair, each one has suffered some break of legs or arms or spindles, while the original remains as firm in its withered old age as it was the day I rescued it from the " out-kitchen " of the Long Island farm-house.

For the next fifty years after the close of our colonial history, the colonial cabinet-makers in New England and the northern Middle States continued to flourish, evolving an occasional good variation from what may be called colonial forms. Rush- and flag-bottomed chairs and chairs with seats of twisted rawhide—the frames often gilded and painted—

sometimes took the place of wrought
mahogany, except in the best rooms
of great houses. Many of these are
of excellent shape and construction,
and specially interesting as an adaptation of natural products of the
country. Undoubtedly, with our ingenious modern appliances, we could
make as good furniture as was made
in Chippendale and Sheraton's day,
with far less expenditure of effort;
but the demon of competition in
trade will not allow it. We must
use all material, perfect or imperfect;
we cannot afford to select. We must
cover knots and imperfections with
composition and pass them on. We
must use the cheapest glue, and save
an infinitesimal sum in the length of
our dowels; we must varnish instead
of polishing, or "the other man" will
get the better of us. If we did not
do these things our furniture would
be better, but "the other man"

would sell more, because he could sell more cheaply.

Since the revived interest in the making of furniture, we find an occasional and marked recurrence to primitive form——on each occasion the apparently new style taking on the name of the man who produced it.

In our own day we have seen the "Eastlake furniture" appear and disappear, succeeded by the "Morris furniture," which is undoubtedly better adapted to our varied wants. At present, mortising and dowelling have come to the front as proper processes, especially for table-building; and this time the style appears under the name of "Mission furniture." Much of this is extremely well suited for cottage furnishing, but the occasional exaggeration of the style takes one back not only to early, but the earliest, English art, when chairs were immovable seats or blocks, and tables absolute fixtures on account of the weighty legs upon which they were built. In short, the careful and cultivated decorator finds it as imperative to guard against exaggerated simplicity as unsupported prettiness.

Fortunately there has been a great deal of attention paid to good cabinet work within the last few years, and although the method of its making lacks the human motive and the human interest of former days—it is still a good expression of the art of to-day, and at its best, worthy to be carried down with the generations as one of the steps in the evolutions of time. What we have to do, is to learn to discriminate between good and bad, to appreciate the best in design and workmanship, even although we cannot afford to buy it. In this case we should learn to do with less. As a rule our houses are crowded.

If we are able to buy a few good things, we are apt instead to buy many only moderately good, for lavish possession seems to be a sort of passion, or birthright, of Americans. It follows that we fill our houses with heterogeneous collections of furniture, new and old, good and bad, appropriate or inappropriate, as the case may be, with a result of living in seeming luxury, but a luxury without proper selection or true value. To have less would in many cases be to have more—more tranquillity of life, more ease of mind, more knowledge and more real enjoyment.

There is another principle which can be brought into play in this case, and that is the one of buying—not a costly kind of thing, but the best of its kind. If it is a choice in chairs, for instance, let it be the best cane-seated, or rush-bottomed chair that is made, instead of the second or third

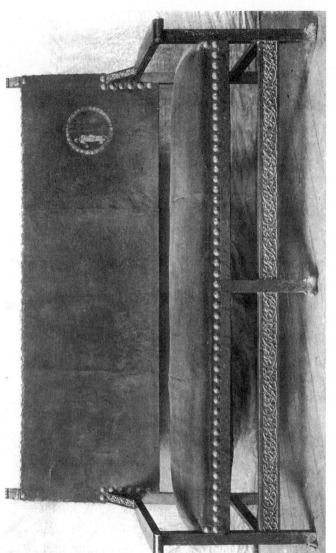

SOFA DESIGNED BY MRS. CANDACE WHEELER FOR N.Y. LIBRARY IN "WOMAN'S BUILDING," COLUMBIAN EXPOSITION

best upholstered or leather-covered one. If it is a question of tables, buy the simplest form made of flawless wood and with best finish, instead of a bargain in elaborately turned or scantily carved material. If it is in bedsteads, a plain brass, or good enamelled iron or a simple form in black walnut, instead of a cheap inlaid wood——and so on through the whole category. A good chintz or cotton is better for draperies, than flimsy silk or brocade; and when all is done the very spirit of truth will sit enthroned in the household, and we shall find that all things have been brought into harmony by her laws.

Although the furnishing of a house should be one of the most painstaking and studied of pursuits, there is certainly nothing which is at the same time so fascinating and so flattering in its promise of future enjoyment. It is like the making of a picture as far as possibility of beauty is concerned, but a picture within and against which one's life, and the life of the family, is to be lived. It is a bit of creative art in itself, and one which concerns us so closely as to be a very part of us. We enjoy every separate thing we may find or select or procure—not only for the beauty and goodness which is in it, but for its contribution to the general whole. And in knowledge of applied and manufactured art, the furnishing of a house is truly "the beginning of wisdom." One learns to appreciate what is excellent in the new, from study and appreciation of quality in the old.

It is the fascination of this study which has made a multiplication of shops and collections of "antiques" in every quarter of the city. Many a woman begins from the shop-

keeper's point of view of the value
of mere age, and learns by experience
that age, considered by itself, is a dis-
qualification, and that it gives value
only when the art which created the
antique has been lost or greatly de-
teriorated. If one can find as good,
or a better thing in art and quality,
made to-day—by all means buy the
thing of to-day, and let yourself and
your children be credited with the
hundred or two years of wear which
is in it. We can easily see that it is
wiser to buy modern iridescent glass,
fitted to our use, and yet carrying all
the fascinating lustre of ancient glass,
than to sigh for the possession of some
unbuyable thing belonging to dead
and gone Cæsars. And the case is
as true of other modern art and
modern inventions, if the art is good,
and the inventions suitable to our
wants and needs.

Yet in spite of the goodness of

much that is new, there is a subtle
pleasure in turning over, and even in
appropriating, the things that are old.
There are certain fenced-in-blocks
on the east side of New York City
where for many years the choice parts
of old houses have been deposited.
As fashion and wealth have changed
their locality — treading slowly up
from the Battery to Central Park—
many beautiful bits of construction
have been left behind in the aban-
doned houses—either disregarded on
account of change in popular taste,
or unappreciated by reason of want
of knowledge. For the few whose
knowledge was competent, there
were things to be found in the sec-
ond-hand yards, precious beyond
comparison with anything of con-
temporaneous manufacture.

There were panelled front doors
with beautifully fluted columns and

carved capitals, surmounted by half-ovals of curiously designed sashes; there were beautifully wrought iron railings, and elaborate newel-posts of mahogany, brass door-knobs and hinges, and English hob-grates, and crystal chandeliers of cost and brilliance, and panelled wainscots of oak and mahogany; chimney-pieces in marble and wood of an excellence which we are almost vainly trying to compass, and all of them to be bought at the price of lumber.

These are the things to make one who remembers them critical about the collections to be found in the antique shops of to-day, and yet such shops are enticing and fashionable, and the quest of antiques will go on until we become convinced of the art-value and the equal merit of the new — which period many things seem to indicate is not far off.

In those days there was but one
antique shop in all New York which
was devoted to the sale of old things,
to furniture, pictures, statuary, and
what Ruskin calls "portable art" of
all kinds.   It was a place where one
might go, crying " new lamps for old
ones" with a certainty of profit in
the transaction.   In later years it has
been known as *Sypher's*, and although
one of many, instead of a single one,
is still a place of fascinating possibilities.

To sum up the gospel of furnishing, we need only fall back upon the
principles of absolute fitness, actual
goodness, and real beauty.   If the
furniture of a well-coloured room
possesses these three qualities, the
room as a whole can hardly fail to be
lastingly satisfactory.   It must be remembered, however, that it is a trin-
ity of virtues.   No piece of furniture
should be chosen because it is intrin-

sically good or genuinely beautiful, if it has not also its *use*—and this rule applies to all rooms, with the one exception of the drawing-room.

The necessity of *use*, governing the style of furnishing in a room, is very well understood. Thus, while both drawing-room and dining-room must express hospitality, it is of a different kind or degree. That of the drawing-room is ceremonious and punctilious, and represents the family in its relation to society, while the dining-room is far more intimate, and belongs to the family in its relation to friends. In fact, as the dining-room is the heart of the house, its furnishing would naturally be quite different in feeling and character from the drawing-room, although it might be fully as lavish in cost. It would be stronger, less conservative, and altogether more personal in its expression. Family portraits and family silver give the personal note which we like to recognise in our friends' dining-rooms, because the intimacy of the room makes even family history in place.

In moderate houses, even the drawing-room is too much a family room to allow it to be entirely emancipated from the law of use, but in houses which are not circumscribed in space, and where one or more rooms are set apart to social rather than domestic life, it is natural and proper to gather in them things which stand, primarily, for art and beauty—which satisfy the needs of the mind as distinct from those of bodily comfort. Things which belong in the category of "unrelated beauty" may be appropriately gathered in such a room, because the use of it is to please the eye and excite the interest of our social world; therefore a table which is a marvel of art, but not of convenience, or a casket which is beautiful to look at, but of no practical use, are in accordance with the idea of the room. They help compose a picture, not only for the eyes of friends and acquaintances, but for the education of the family.

It follows that an artistic and luxurious drawing-room may be a true family expression; it may speak of travel and interest in the artistic development of mankind; but even where the experiences of the family have been wide and liberal, if the house and circumstances are narrow, a luxurious interior is by no means a happiness.

It may seem quite superfluous to give advice against luxury in furnishing except where it is warranted by exceptional means, because each family naturally adjusts its furnishing to its own needs and circumstances; but the influence of mere beauty is very powerful, and many a costly toy drifts into homes where it does not rightly belong, and where, instead of being an educational or elevating influence, it is a source of mental deterioration, from its conflict with unsympathetic circumstances. A long and useful chapter might be written upon "art out of place," but nothing which could be said upon the subject would apply to that incorporation of art and beauty with furniture and interior surroundings, which is the effort and object of every true artist and art-lover.

The fact to be emphasised is, that *objets d'art*—beautiful in themselves and costly because of the superior knowledge, artistic feeling, and patient labour which have produced them—demand care and reserve for their preservation, which is not available in a household where the first motive of everything must be ministry to comfort. Art in the shape of pictures is fortunately exempt from this rule, and may dignify and beautify every room in the house without being imperilled by contact in the exigencies of use.

Following out this idea, a house where circumstances demand that there shall be no drawing-room, and where the family sitting-room must also answer for the reception of guests, a perfect beauty and dignity may be achieved by harmony of colour, beauty of form, and appropriateness to purpose, and this may be carried to almost any degree of perfection by the introduction and accompaniment of pictures. In this case art is a part of the room, as well as an adornment of it. It is kneaded into every article of furniture. It is the daily bread of art to which we are all entitled, and which can make a small country home, or a smaller

city apartment, as enjoyable and elevating as if it were filled with the
luxuries of art.

But one may say, "It requires
knowledge to do this; much knowledge in the selection of the comparatively few things which are to make
up such an interior," and that is
true—and the knowledge is to be
proved every time we come to the
test of buying. Yet it is a curious
fact that the really *good* thing, the
thing which is good in art as well as
construction, will inevitably be chosen
by an intelligent buyer, instead of
the thing which is bad in art and in
construction. Fortunately, one can
see good examples in the shops of
to-day, where twenty years ago at
best only honest and respectable furniture was on exhibition. One must
rely somewhat on the character of
the places from which one buys,
and not expect good styles and relia-

RUSTIC SOFA AND TABLES IN "PENNYROYAL" (IN MRS. BOUDINOT KEITH'S COTTAGE, ONTEORA)

ble manufacture where commercial success is the dominant note of the business. In truth the careful buyer is not so apt to fail in quality as in harmony, because grade as well as style in different articles and manufactures is to be considered. What is perfectly good in one grade of manufacture will not be in harmony with a higher or lower grade in another. Just as we choose our grade of floor-covering from ingrain to Aubusson, we must choose the grade of other furnishings. Even an inexperienced buyer would be apt to feel this, and would know that if she found a simple ingrain-filling appropriate to a bed-chamber, maple or enamelled furniture would belong to it, instead of more costly inlaid or carved pieces.

It may be well to reiterate the fact that the predominant use of each room in a house gives the clew to the best rules of treatment in decoration and furniture. For instance, the hall, being an intermediate space between in and out of doors, should be coloured and furnished in direct reference to this, and to its common use as a thoroughfare by all members of the family. It is not a place of prolonged occupation, and may therefore properly be without the luxury and ease of lounges and lounging-chairs. But as long as it serves both as entrance-room to the house and for carrying the stairways to the upper floors, it should be treated in such a way as to lead up to and prepare the mind for whatever of inner luxury there may be in the house. At the same time it should preserve something of the simplicity and freedom from all attempt at effect which belong to out-of-door life. The difference between its decoration and furniture and that of other divisions of the house should be principally in surface, and not in colour. Difference of surface is secured by the use of materials which are permanent and durable in effect, such as wood, plaster, and leather. These may all be coloured without injury to their impression of permanency, although it is generally preferable to take advantage of indigenous or "inherent colour" like the natural yellows and russets of wood and leather. When these are used for both walls and ceiling, it will be found that, to give the necessary variation, and prevent an impression of monotony and dulness, some tint must be added in the ornament of the surface, which could be gained by a forcible deepening or variation of the general tone, like a deep golden brown, which is the lowest tone of the scale of yellow, or a red which would be only a variant of the prevailing tint. The introduction of an opposing or contrasting tint, like pale blue in small masses as compared with the general tint, even if it is in so small a space as that of a water-colour on the wall, adds the necessary contrast, and enlivens and invigorates a harmony.

No colour carries with it a more appropriate influence at the entrance of a house than red in its different values.   Certain tints of it which are known both as Pompeiian and Damascus red have sufficient yellow in their composition to fall in with the yellows of oiled wood, and give the charm of a variant but related colour. In its stronger and deeper tones it is in direct contrast to the green of abundant foliage, and therefore a good colour for the entrance-hall or vestibule of a country-house; while the paler tones, which run into pinks, hold the same opposing relation to the gray and blue of the sea-shore.

If walls and ceiling are of wood, a
rug of which the prevailing colour is
red will often give the exact note
which is needed to preserve the room
from monotony and insipidity. A
stair-carpet is a valuable point to
make in a hall, and it is well to reserve all opposing colour for this one
place, which, as it rises, meets all
sight on a level, and makes its contrast directly and unmistakably. A
stair-carpet has other reasons for use
in a country-house than æsthetic
ones, as the stairs are conductors of
sound to all parts of the house, and
should therefore be muffled, and because a carpeted stair furnishes much
safer footing for the two family extremes of childhood and age.

The furniture of the hall should
not be fantastic, as some cabinet-
makers seem to imagine. Impossible
twists in the supports of tables and
chairs are perhaps more objectionable

in this first vestibule or entrance to the house than elsewhere, because the mind is not quite free from out-of-door influences, or ready to take pleasure in the vagaries of the human fancy. Simple chairs, settles, and tables, more solid perhaps than is desirable in other parts of the house, are what the best natural, as well as the best cultivated, taste demands. If there is one place more than another where a picture performs its full work of suggestion and decoration, it is in a hall which is otherwise bare of ornament. Pictures in dining-rooms make very little impression as pictures, because the mind is engrossed with the first and natural purpose of the room, and consequently not in a waiting and easily impressible mood; but in a hall, if one stops for even a moment, the thoughts are at leisure, and waiting to be interested. Aside from the

colour effect, which may be so managed as to be very valuable, pictures
hung in a hall are full of suggestion
of wider mental and physical life, and,
like books, are indications of the
tastes and experiences of the family.
Of course there are country-houses
where the halls are built with fireplaces, and windows commanding
favourite views, and are really intended for family sitting-rooms and
gathering-places; in this case it is
generally preceded by a vestibule
which carries the character of an entrance-hall, leaving the large room
to be furnished more luxuriously, as
is proper to a sitting-room.

The dining-room shares with the
hall a purpose common to the life of
the family, and, while it admits of
much more variety and elaboration,
that which is true of the hall is
equally true of the dining-room, that
it should be treated with materials

which are durable and have surface quality, although its decoration should be preferably with china rather than with pictures. It is important that the colour of a dining-room should be pervading colour — that is, that walls and ceiling should be kept together by the use of one colour only, in different degrees of strength.

For many reasons, but principally because it is the best material to use in a dining-room, the rich yellows of oiled wood make the most desirable colour and surface. The rug, the curtains, the portières and screen, can then be of any good tint which the exposure of the room and the decoration of the china seem to indicate. If it has a cold, northern exposure, reds or gold browns are indicated; but if it is a sunny and warm-looking room, green or strong India blue will be found more satisfactory in simple houses. The materials used in cur-

tains, portières, and screens should be
of cotton or linen, or some plain
woollen goods which are as easily
washable. A one-coloured, heavy-
threaded cotton canvas, a linen in
solid colour, or even indigo-blue domestic, all make extremely effective
and appropriate furnishings. The
variety of blue domestic which is
called denim is the best of all fabrics
for this kind of furnishing, if the colour is not too dark.

The prettiest country house dining-room I know is ceiled and wain-
scoted with wood, the walls above
the wainscoting carrying an ingrain
paper of the same tone; the line of
division between the wainscot and
wall being broken by a row of old
blue India china plates, arranged in
groups of different sizes and running
entirely around the room. There is
one small mirror set in a broad
carved frame of yellow wood hung

in the centre of a rather large wall-space, its angles marked by small Dutch plaques; but the whole decoration of the room outside of these pieces consists of draperies of blue denim in which there is a design, in narrow white outline, of leaping fish, and the widening water-circles and showery drops made by their play. The white lines in the design answer to the white spaces in the decorated china, and the two used together in profusion have an unexpectedly decorative effect. The table and chairs are, of course, of the same coloured wood used in the ceiling and wainscot, and the rug is an India cotton of dark and light blues and white. The sideboard is an arrangement of fixed shelves, but covered with a beautiful collection of blue china, which serves to furnish the table as well. If the dining-room had a northern exposure, and it was desira-

DINING-ROOM IN "STAR ROCK" (COUNTRY HOUSE OF W. E. CONNOR, ESQ. ONTEORA)

ble to use red instead of blue for
colouring, as good an effect could be
secured by depending for ornament
upon the red Kaga porcelain so common at present in Japanese and Chi-
nese shops, and using with it the
Eastern cotton known as *bez*. This
is dyed with madder, and exactly
repeats the red of the porcelain, while
it is extremely durable both in colour and texture. Borders of yellow
stitchery, or straggling fringes of silk
and beads, add very much to the
effect of the drapery and to the character of the room.

A library in ordinary family life
has two parts to play. It is not
only to hold books, but to make the
family at home in a literary atmosphere. Such a room is apt to be a
fascinating one by reason of this
very variety of use and purpose,
and because it is a centre for all
the family treasures. Books, pictures,

papers, photographs, bits of decorative needlework, all centre here, and all are on most orderly behaviour, like children at a company dinner. The colour of such a room may, and should, be much warmer and stronger than that of a parlour pure and simple, the very constancy and hardness of its use indicating tints of strength and resistance; but, keeping that in mind, the rules for general use of colour and harmony of tints will apply as well to a room used for a double purpose as for a single. Of course the furniture should be more solid and darker, as would be necessary for constant use, but the deepening of tones in general colour provides for that, and for the use of rugs of a different character. In a room of this kind perhaps the best possible effect is produced by the use of some textile as a wall-covering, as in that case the same material with a contrasted colour in the lining can be used for curtains, and to some extent in the furniture. This use of one material has not only an effect of richness which is due to the library of the house, but it softens and brings together all the heterogeneous things which different members of a large family are apt to require in a sitting-room.

To those who prefer to work out and adapt their own surroundings, it is well to illustrate the advice given for colour in different exposures by selecting particular rooms, with their various relations to light, use, and circumstances, and seeing how colour-principles can be applied to them.

We may choose a reception-hall, in either a city or country house, since the treatment would in both cases be guided by the same rules. If in a city house, it may be on the shady or the sunny side of the street,

and this at once would differentiate,
perhaps the colour, and certainly the
depth of colour to be used. If it
is the hall of a country house the
difference between north or south
light will not be as great, since a
room opening on the north in a
house standing alone, in unobstructed
space, would have an effect of coldness, but not necessarily of shadow or
darkness. The first condition, then,
of coldness of light would have to be
considered in both cases, but less
positively in the country, than in the
city house. If the room is actually
dark, a warm or orange tone of yellow will both modify and lighten it.

Gold-coloured or yellow canvas
with oak mouldings lighten and warm
the walls; and rugs with a prepon-
derance of white and yellow trans-
form a dark hall into a light and
cheerful one. It must be remembered that few dark colours can

assert themselves in the absolute
shadow of a north light. Green and
blue become black. Gold, orange,
and red alone have sufficient power
to hold their own, and make us conscious of them in darkness.

In a hall which has plenty of
light, but no sun, red is an effective
and natural colour, copper-coloured
leather paper, cushions and rugs or
carpets of varying shades of red,
and transparent curtains of the same
tint give an effect of warmth and
vitality. Red is truly a delightful
colour to deal with in shadowed
interiors, its sensitiveness to light,
changing from colour-tinted darkness to palpitating ruby, and even to
flame colour, on the slightest invita-
tion of day- or lamp-light, makes it
like a living presence. It is especially valuable at the entrance of the
home, where it seems to meet one
with almost a human welcome.

If we can succeed in making what would be a cold and unattractive entrance hospitable and cordial by liberal use of warm and strong colour, by reversing the effort we can just as easily modify the effect of glaring, or overpowering, sunlight.

Suppose the entrance-hall of the house to be upon the sunny side of the street, where in addition to the natural effect of full rays of the sun there are also the reflections from innumerable other house-fronts and house-windows.

In this case we must simulate shadow and mystery, and this can be done by the colour-tones of blues and greens. I use these in the plural because the shadows of both are innumerable, and because all, except perhaps turquoise and apple-green, are natural shadow-tints. Green and blue can be used together or separately, according to the skill and

what is called the " colour-sense "
with which they are applied.

To use them together requires not
only observation of colour-occurrences
in nature but sensitiveness to the more
subtle out-of-door effects, resulting
from intermingling of shadows and
reflection of lights. Well done, it is
one of the most beautiful and satisfactory of achievements, but it may easily
be bad by reason of sharp contrasts, or
unmodified juxtaposition.

But a room where blue in all its
shades from dark to light alone predominates, or a room where only
green is used, bright and gray tones
in contrast and variation is within
the reach of most colour-loving mor-
tals, and as both of these tints are
companionable with oak and gold,
and to be found in nearly all decoration materials, it is easy to arrange
a refined and beautiful effect in either
colour.

It will require little reflection to show that a hall skilfully treated with green or blue tints would modify the colour of sunlight, without giving a sense of discord. It would be like passing only from sunlight to grateful shadow, and this because in all art the actual representation shadow-colour would be blue or green. The shadow of a tree falling upon snow on a sunny winter day is blue. The shadow of a sunheated rock in summer is green, and the success of either of these schemes of decoration would be because of adherence to an actual principle of colour, or a knowledge of the peculiar qualities of certain colours and their proper use. It would be an intelligent application of the medicinal or healing qualities of colour to the constitution of the house, as skilful physicians use medicines to overcome constitutional defects or difficulties in man.

This may be called *corrective* treatment of a room, and may, of course, include all the decorative devices of ornament, design and furniture, and although it is not, strictly speaking, decoration, it should certainly and always precede decoration.

It is sad to see an elaborate scheme of ornament based upon bad colour-treatment, and unfortunately this not infrequently happens.

It is difficult to give a formula for the decoration of any room in relation to its colour-treatment, except by a careful description of certain successful examples, each one of which illustrates principles that may be of use to the amateur or student of the art.

One which occurs to me in this immediate connection is a dining-room in an apartment house, where this room alone is absolutely without what may be called exterior light.

Its two windows open upon a well,
the brick wall of which is scarcely
ten feet away.   Fortunately, it makes
a part of the home of a much travelled and exceedingly cultivated pair
of beings, the business of one being
to create beauty in the way of pictures and the other of statues, so perhaps it is less than a wonder that this
square, unattractive well-room should
have blossomed under their hands
into a dining-room perfect in colour,
style, and fittings.   I shall give only
the result, the process being capable
of infinite small variations.

At present it is a room sixteen feet
square, one side of which is occupied
by two nearly square windows.   The
wood-work, including a five-foot
wainscot of small square panels, is
painted a glittering varnished white
which is warm in tone, but not
creamy.   The upper halves of the
square windows are of semi-opaque

yellow glass, veined and variable, but clear enough everywhere to admit a stained yellow light. Below these, thin yellow silk curtains cross each other, so that the whole window-space radiates yellow light. If we reflect that the colour of sunlight is yellow, we shall be able to see both the philosophy and the result of this treatment.

The wall above the wainscot is covered with a plain unbleached muslin, stencilled at the top in a re-peating design of faint yellow tile-like squares which fade gradually into white at a foot below the ceiling. At intervals along the wall are water-colours of flat Holland meadows, or blue canals, balanced on either side by a blue delft plate, and in a corner near the window is a veritable blue porcelain stove, which once faintly warmed some far-off German in-terior. The floor is polished oak, as are the table and chairs. I purposely leave out all the accessories and devices of brass and silver, the quaint brass-framed mirrors, the ivy-encircled windows, the one or two great ferns, the choice blue table-furniture:—because these are personal and should neither be imitated or reduced to rules.

The lesson is in the use of yellow and white, accented with touches of blue, which converts a dark and perfectly cheerless room into a glitter of light and warmth.

The third example I shall give is of a dining-room which may be called palatial in size and effect, occupying the whole square wing of a well-known New York house. There are many things in this house in the way of furniture, pictures, historic bits of art in different lines, which would distinguish it among fine houses, but one particular room is, perhaps, as

perfectly successful in richness of detail, picturesqueness of effect, and at
the same time perfect appropriateness
to time, place, and circumstances as
is possible for any achievement of its
kind. The dining-room, and its art,
taken in detail, belongs to the Venetian school, but if its colour-effect
were concentrated upon canvas, it
would be known as a Rembrandt.
There is the same rich shadow, covering a thousand gradations,—the same
concentration of light, and the same
liberal diffusion of warm and rich
tones of colour. It is a grand room
in space, as New York interiors go,
being perhaps forty to fifty feet in
breadth and length, with a height
exactly proportioned to the space.
It has had the advantage of separate
creation—being "thought out" years
after the early period of the house,
and is, consequently, a concrete result of study, travel, and oppor-

tunities, such as few families are
privileged to experience. Aside from
the perfect proportions of the room,
it is not difficult to analyse the art
which makes it so distinguished an
example of decoration of space, and
decide wherein lies its especial charm.
It is undoubtedly that of colour, although this is based upon a detail so
perfect, that one hesitates to give it
predominant credit. The whole, or
nearly the whole west end of the
room is thrown into one vast, slightly
projecting window of clear leaded
glass, the lines of which stand against
the light like a weaving of spiders'
webs. There is a border of various
tints at its edge, which softens it into
the brown shadow of the room, and
the centre of each large sash is marked
by a shield-like ornament glowing
with colour like a jewel. The long
ceiling and high wainscoting melt
away from this leaded window in

DINING-ROOM IN NEW YORK HOUSE SHOWING LEADED-GLASS WINDOWS

a perspective of wonderfully carved planes of antique oak, catching the light on lines and points of projection and quenching it in hollows of relief.

These perpendicular wall panels were scaled from a room in a Venetian palace, carved when the art and the fortunes of that sea-city were at their best, and the alternately repeating squares of the ceiling were fashioned to carry out and supplement the ancient carvings. If this were a small room, there would be a sense of unrest in so lavish a use of broken surface, but in one large enough to have it felt as a whole, and not in detail, it simply gives a quality of preciousness. The soft browns of the wood spread a mystery of surface, from the edge of the polished floor until it meets a frieze of painted canvas filled with large reclining figures clad in draperies of red, and blue, and yellow——separating the walls from the ceiling by an illumination of colour. This colour-decoration belongs to the past, and it is a question if any modern painting could have adapted itself so perfectly to the spirit of the room, although in itself it might be far more beautiful. It is a bit of antique imagination, its cherub-borne plates of fruit, and golden flagons, and brown-green of foliage and turquoise of sky, and crimson and gold of garments, all softened to meet the shadows of the room. The door-spaces in the wainscot are hung with draperies of crimson velvet, the surface frayed and flattened by time into variations of red, impossible to newer weavings, while the great floor-space is spread with an enormous rug of the same colour—the gift of a Sultan. A carved table stands in the centre, surrounded with high-backed carved chairs, the seats covered with the

same antique velvet which shows in
the portières. A fall of thin crimson
silk tints the sides of the window-
frame, and on the two ends of the
broad step or platform which leads to
the window stand two tall pedestals
and globe-shaped jars of red and
blue-green pottery. The deep, ruby-
like red of the one and the mixed
indefinite tint of the other seem to
have curdled into the exact shade for
each particular spot, their fitness is so
perfect.

The very sufficient knowledge
which has gone to the making of this
superb room has kept the draperies
unbroken by design or device, giving
colour only and leaving to the carved
walls the privilege of ornament.

It will be seen that there are but
two noticeable colour-tones in the
room—brown with infinite variations,
and red in rugs and draperies.

There is no real affinity between

these two tints, but they are here so
well balanced in mass, that the two
form a complete harmony, like the
brown waves of a landscape at even,
ing tipped with the fire of a sunset
sky.

Much is to be learned from a
room like this, in the lesson of unity
and concentration of effect. The
strongest, and in fact the only, mass
of vital colour is in the carpet, which
is allowed to play upwards, as it were,
into draperies, and furniture, and
frieze, none of which show the same
depth and intensity. To the concentration of light in the one great window we must give the credit of the
Rembrandt-like effect of the whole
interior. If the walls were less rich,
this single flood of light would be a
defect, because it would be difficult
to treat a plain surface with colour
alone, which should be equally good
in strong light and deep shadow.

DINING-ROOM IN NEW YORK HOME SHOWING CARVED WAINSCOTING AND PAINTED FRIEZE

Then, again, the amount of living
and brilliant colour is exactly proportioned to that of sombre brown,
the red holding its value by strength,
as against the greatly preponderating
mass of dark. On the whole this
may be called a " picture-room," and
yet it is distinctly liveable, lending
itself not only to hospitality and
ceremonious function but also to
real domesticity. It is true that
there is a certain obligation in its
style of beauty which calls for fine
manners and fine behaviour, possibly
even, behaviour in kind; for it is in
the nature of all fine and exceptional
things to demand a corresponding
fineness from those who enjoy them.

I will give still another dining-
room as an example of colour, which,
unlike the others, is not modern, but
a sort of falling in of old gentility
and costliness into lines of modern
art—one might almost say it *hap-*

pened to be beautiful, and yet the happening is only an adjustment of fine old conditions to modern ideas. Yet I have known many as fine a room torn out and refitted, losing thereby all the inherent dignity of age and superior associations.

A beautiful city home of seventy years ago is not very like a beautiful city home of to-day; perhaps less so in this than in any other country. The character of its fineness is curiously changed; the modern house is fitted to its inmates, while the old-fashioned house, modelled upon the early eighteenth century art of England, obliged the inmates to fit themselves as best they might to a given standard.

The dining-room I speak of belongs to the period when Washington Square, New York, was still surrounded by noble homes, and almost the limit of luxurious city life was

Union Square. The house fronts to
the north, consequently the dining-
room, which is at the back, is flooded
with sunshine. The ceiling is higher
than it would be in a modern house,
and the windows extend to the floor,
and rise nearly to the ceiling, far indeed above the flat arches of the
doorways with their rococo flourishes.
This extension of window-frame, and
the heavy and elaborate plaster cornice so deep as to be almost a frieze,
and the equally elaborate centre-
piece, are the features which must
have made it a room difficult to
ameliorate.

I could fancy it must have been
an ugly room in the old days when
its walls were probably white, and
the great mahogany doors were spots
of colour in prevailing spaces of
blankness. Now, however, any one
at all learned in art, or sensitive to
beauty, would pronounce it a beau-

tiful room. The way in which the
ceiling with its heavy centre-piece and
plaster cornice is treated is especially interesting. The whole of this
is covered with an ochre-coloured
bronze, while the walls and door-
casings are painted a dark indigo,
which includes a faint trace of green.
Over this wall-colour, and joining
the cornice, is carried a stencil design in two coloured bronzes which
seem to repeat the light and shadow
of the cornice mouldings, and this
apparently extends the cornice into a
frieze which ends faintly at a picture-
moulding some three feet below.
This treatment not only lowers the
ceiling, which is in construction too
high for the area of the room, but
blends it with the wall in a way
which imparts a certain richness of
effect to all the lower space.

The upper part of the windows,
to the level of the picture-moulding,

is covered with green silk, overlaid with an appliqué of the same in a design somewhat like the frieze, so that it seems to carry the frieze across the space of light in a green tracery of shadow. The same green extends from curtain-rods at the height of the picture-moulding into long under-curtains of silk, while the over-curtains are of indigo coloured silk-canvas which matches the walls.

The portières separating the dining-room from the drawing-room are of a wonderfully rich green brocade —the colour of which answers to the green of the silk under-curtains across the room, while the design ranges itself indisputably with the period of the plaster work. The blue and green of the curtains and portière each seem to claim their own in the mixed and softened background of the wall.

The colour of the room would

hardly be complete without the three beautiful portraits which hang upon the walls, and suggest their part of the life and conversation of to-day so that it stands on a proper plane with the dignity of three generations. The beautiful mahogany doors and elaboration of cornice and central ornament belong to them, but the harmony and beauty of colour are of our own time and tell of the general knowledge and feeling for art which belongs to it.

I have given the colour-treatment only of this room, leaving out the effect of carved teak-wood furniture and subtleties of china and glass— not alone as an instance of colour in a sunny exposure, but as an example of fitting new styles to old, of keeping what is valuable and beautiful in itself and making it a part of the comparatively new art of decoration.

There is a dining-room in one of

GLASS BY DUNHAM WHEELER

SCREEN BY DORA WHEELER KEITH

SCREEN AND GLASS WINDOW IN HOUSE AT LAKEWOOD
(BELONGING TO CLARENCE ROOF, ESQ.)

the many delightful houses in Lakewood, N. J., which owes its unique
charm to a combination of position,
light, colour, and perhaps more than
all, to the clever decoration of its
upper walls, which is a fine and broad
composition of swans and many-col-
oured clusters of grapes and vine-
foliage placed above the softly
tinted copper-coloured wall. The
same design is carried in silvery and
gold-coloured leaded-glass across the
top of the wide west window, as
shown in illustration opposite page
2 2 2, and reappears with a shield-
shaped arrangement of wings in a
beautiful four-leaved screen.

The notable and enjoyable colour
of the room is seen from the very
entrance of the house, the broad
main hall making a carpeted highway
to the wide opening of the room,
where a sheaf of tinted sunset light
seems to spread itself like a many-

doubled fan against the shadows of the hall.

All the ranges and intervals, the lights, reflections, and darks possible to that most beautiful of metals— copper—seem to be gathered into the frieze and screen, and melt softly into the greens of the foliage, or tint the plumage of the swans. It is an instance of the kind of decoration which is both classic and domestic, and being warmed and vivified by beautiful colour, appeals both to the senses and the imagination.

It would be easy to multiply instances of beautiful rooms, and each one might be helpful for mere imitation, but those I have given have each one illustrated—more or less distinctly—the principle of colour as affecting or being affected by light.

I have not thought it necessary to give examples of rooms with eastern or western exposures, because in such rooms one is free to consult one's own personal preferences as to colour, being limited only by the general rules which govern all colour decoration.

I have not spoken of pictures or paintings as accessories of interior decoration, because while their influence upon the character and degree of beauty in the house is greater than all other things put together, their selection and use are so purely personal as not to call for remark or advice. Any one who loves pictures well enough to buy them, can hardly help placing them where they not only are at their best, but where they will also have the greatest influence.

A house where pictures predominate will need little else that comes under the head of decoration. It is a pity that few houses have this advantage, but fortunately it is quite

possible to give a picture quality to
every interior. This can often be
done by following the lead of some
accidental effect which is in itself
picturesque. The placing a jar of
pottery or metal near or against a
piece of drapery which repeats its
colour and heightens the lustre of its
substance is a small detail, but one
which gives pleasure out of all proportion to its importance. The half
accidental draping of a curtain, the
bringing together of shapes and colours in insignificant things, may give
a character which is lastingly pleasing
both to inmates and casual visitors.

Of course this is largely a matter
of personal gift. One person may
make a picturesque use of colour and
material, which in the hands of another will be perhaps without fault,
but equally without charm. Instances of this kind come constantly
within our notice, although we are

not always able to give the exact reasons for success or failure. We only know that we feel the charm of one instance and are indifferent to, or totally unimpressed by, the other.

It is by no means an unimportant thing to create a beautiful and picturesque interior. There is no influence so potent upon life as harmonious surroundings, and to create and possess a home which is harmonious in a simple and inexpensive way is the privilege of all but the wretchedly poor. In proportion also as these surroundings become more perfect in their art and meaning, there is a corresponding elevation in the dweller among them—since the best decoration must include many spiritual lessons. It may indeed be used to further vulgar ambitions, or pamper bodily weaknesses, but truth and beauty are its essentials, and these will have their utterance.